CROCHET *Cute Critters*

CROCHET
Cute Critters

26 EASY
Amigurumi Patterns

Sarah Zimmerman

ROCKRIDGE
PRESS

Cover and interior Designer: Merideth Harte
Photo Art Director/Art Manager: Sarah Feinstein
Editors: Meg Ilasco, Salwa Jabado
Production Editor: Ashley Polikoff
Photography © 2019 Evi Abeler, cover, p. ii, vi-viii, x, 24, 26, 30, 34, 38, 42, 46, 50, 54, 58, 62, 64, 68, 72, 76, 80, 83-84, 88, 92, 96, 100, 104, 108, 110, 114, 118, 122; Sarah Zimmerman, p. 6-12, 15, 17-19, 21, 23. Prop styling by Albane Sharrard.
Author Photographer: Melissa DeMers | Lissarie Photography

ISBN: Print 978-1-64152-230-4 | eBook 978-1-64152-231-1

R1

For Micah, Chase, and Zoe. My kids, my world, and my inspiration behind all of my crochet designs. And for my husband, Joel, who has always been my biggest supporter.

Contents

ALEX THE
Alligator

BENNY THE
Bear

CALLIE THE
Cat

DASH THE
Dog

EDWARD THE
Elephant

FREDDY THE
Fox

GINGER THE
Giraffe

HENRIETTA THE
Hippo

IGGY THE
Iguana

JUNIOR THE
Jellyfish

KATIE THE
Kangaroo

LILLY THE
Lamb

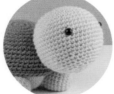

INTRODUCTION

Welcome to the World of Amigurumi!

Pronounced *ah-mee-goo-roo-mee*, this Japanese word may seem like a tongue twister but it simply means the art of crocheting or knitting stuffed toys. The plush animals you will find in this book are actually made from very basic crochet shapes. With just a bit of increasing and decreasing simple stitches, you can make a variety of different animals!

I started crocheting in 2010 after my second son was born. I wanted to make fun and cute hats, toys, and wearables for my babies. One of the first amigurumi projects I remember making was a set of snowballs so my toddler boys could have an indoor snowball fight! Once I mastered crocheting the basic sphere shape, I quickly progressed into making more complex designs. To this day I still enjoy crocheting plush toys for my kids and seeing their faces light up when they see what I have handmade for them.

In this book, you will find that each crochet animal starts with the same basic pattern. This makes these cute critters beginner-friendly, but you will need to already have knowledge of how to crochet. These patterns use only basic stitches and techniques: single crochet, half double crochet, double crochet, increase and decrease stitches, and a magic ring. You should be familiar with using a tapestry needle and weaving in loose ends.

You will find 26 crochet animal patterns in this book. There is an amigurumi for each letter of the alphabet, starting with Alex the Alligator and ending with Zina the Zebra! Each critter is cuter than the next! All are completely customizable. Once you get started, you will want to make them all!

PART ONE

Getting Started

Let's get started! You will need to gather all your essential crochet tools. Feel free to start with any one of the 26 animals. You will see that once you have made one or two critters, all the others work from the same simple pattern shapes. We will be using worsted weight yarn and a size H crochet hook along with a few other basic supplies that you can easily find at your local craft store or order online. You can make multiple animals from one skein of yarn so pick up a few colors and get your hooks ready!

Essential Tools & Supplies

CROCHET HOOKS

There are many different types of crochet hooks available for purchase. You will find they come in aluminum, steel, plastic, wood, and bamboo. Some have ergonomic handles that are larger or that act as a grip designed to fit more comfortably in your hand. I recommend working with a basic aluminum hook. These are easily available in all craft stores and are very durable. I prefer to use the Susan Bates brand, but many also love Boye hooks. The major difference between these two hooks is that the Bates hooks have an inline throat on the head of the hook where a notch has been cut out as opposed to the Boye hooks that have a tapered head, as you can see in the picture on this page. The inline hooks are typically better for beginner crocheters as they grab the yarn a little more securely and help you keep a smooth tension. But there is no right or wrong choice. Use what is comfortable for you!

Crochet Hook Sizes

You will only need one hook size to make each project in this book: a size **H/8 (5mm) crochet hook**. This is a very commonly used size and works well with worsted weight yarn. There is a handy chart to show the metric conversions. This book uses medium (4) worsted weight yarn; if you will be using other yarn weights, use a hook size one or two sizes smaller than that suggested on the ball band to get the tight stitches desired for these projects.

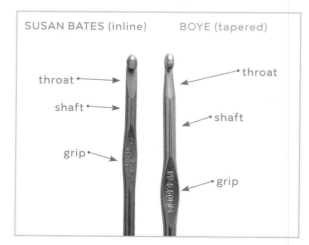

SUSAN BATES (inline)   BOYE (tapered)

throat
shaft
grip

throat
shaft
grip

CROCHET HOOK SIZE	
Metric	US
2.25mm	B-1
2.75mm	C-2
3.25mm	D-3
3.50mm	E-4
3.75mm	F-5
4.00mm	G-6
5.00mm	H-8
5.50mm	I-9
6.00mm	J-10
6.50mm	K-10.5
8.00mm	L-11
9.00mm	M-13
10.00mm	N-15
12.00mm	P-16

STEEL CROCHET HOOK SIZE	
Metric	US
0.50mm	18
0.60mm	16
0.75mm	14
0.85mm	13
1.00mm	12
1.10mm	11
1.25mm	10
1.50mm	8
1.65mm	7
1.75mm	6
1.90mm	5
2.00mm	4

YARN

I have chosen to use Bernat® Super Value™ yarn throughout the entire book. This is a **medium (4) worsted weight yarn** that is available in a huge range of solids, ombres, and heathers. The colors really pop and you get a lot of yardage for the price. It's an acrylic yarn that is machine washable, so it's perfect for amigurumi animals that will be well loved. Every color featured in this book will be used more than once, for more than one cute critter, so you will be able to make the most out of each skein. But feel free to choose any shade of yarn you want for each of the projects. Make them bright or choose a more neutral palette. There are many options and ways to personalize and customize! Bernat Super Value is available for purchase online and in select craft stores. You can also substitute this yarn with another medium (4)

BERNAT® SUPER VALUE™ YARN FEATURES

- Easy care, long-wearing premium acrylic yarn
- Content: 100% acrylic
- Ball size, solids/ragg/heathers: 197g / 7 oz, 389 meters / 426 yards
- Ball Size, ombres: 142g / 5 oz, 251 meters / 275 yards
- Care: Machine wash and dry
- Gauge: (4) worsted
- Crochet gauge: 13 sc and 14 rows with a 5 mm (US H/8) crochet hook

worsted weight yarn.

STUFFING

Poly-fil Premium Polyester Fiber Fill is a high-performance fiberfill that can be used for pillows, dolls, stuffed toys, and crafts. Its fibers have an extraordinary resilience that maintains its integrity when it is washed and dried. It will not bunch! Your amigurumi animals will always keep their shape and stay plush. The Poly-fil brand can be purchased in most craft stores. It's washable, hypoallergenic, and can be machine washed with warm water. Air or tumble dry on low heat. You will need approximately 2 to 3 large 20-ounce bags to complete all of the animals in this book, but it really depends on how much you stuff your critters. The more fiberfill you use, the stiffer the animals will be. Some parts (like Uniqua the Unicorn's horn) should be stuffed more firmly so that they hold their shape.

MATERIALS FOR THE FACE

An easy and adorable option for adding face embellishments to your animal amigurumi is to use **safety eyes and safety noses**. They give a quick finished look to your plush toys. The safety eyes and noses have two parts to them. There is the plastic decorative portion that shows on the outside of your animal and then a washer that snaps over the back, locking each one in place. Once you have locked in your eye or nose, you cannot remove them. They come in a variety of sizes and colors ranging from realistic-looking to classic black. For the projects featured in this book, I used 12mm black safety eyes and 18mm black animal noses. Each of the 26 projects uses one pair of black eyes and a total of six animals use safety noses. Keep in mind that the use of safety eyes and noses is completely optional. As an alternative you can always embroider eyes with black yarn as well as stitch on little triangle noses. Be cautious when using safety eyes and noses for projects that will be given to babies and pets. They are recommended for use for children over the age of three. The most common places to purchase safety eyes and noses are at craft stores or online.

Along with your yarn, crochet hook, stuffing, and safety eyes and noses, there are a few other basic materials that you will need to complete your animal amigurumi. Be sure to have a pair of **scissors** on hand as well as a **medium-size tapestry needle** (also called a darning needle). Unlike sewing needles, tapestry needles have blunt points and large eyes that are ideal for slipping between yarns without snagging or splitting them. You will need a tapestry needle to weave in your ends as well as stitch on embellishments, like the spots on Ginger the Giraffe and the mouth on Lilly the Lamb. A tapestry needle sized anywhere from 17 to 20 will work well with the worsted weight yarn for these projects. You may also want **removable stitch markers**, which can be helpful to mark the beginning of rounds when working in spirals, such as on Edward the Elephant.

Abbreviations

You will need to have a basic understanding of crochet stitches to create these cute critters. They are all made up of simple stitches like the single crochet, half double crochet, and double crochet. For the most part you will just be using the single crochet stitch. The single crochet is commonly used in amigurumi because it creates tight stitches and a solid form (fewer holes and spaces between stitches) that you can stuff without it showing. Below is a crochet stitch abbreviations chart. This book is written in US crochet terms, but the UK conversions are available below.

US Terms	UK Terms
chain = ch	**chain** = ch
stitch = st	**stitch** = st
slip stitch = sl st	**slip stitch** = ss
single crochet = sc	**double crochet** = dc
half double crochet = hdc	**half treble crochet** = htc
double crochet = dc	**treble crochet** = tc
single crochet decrease = sc2tog	**double crochet decrease** = dc2tog

Standard Stitches

SLIP KNOT & CHAIN STITCH (CH)

Typically when you begin a crochet project like a blanket, you will need to start by making a series of chain stitches, called the *foundation chain*. You use this long row of chain stitches as the base to make your first row of crochet stitches into.

In amigurumi projects, like the animals you find in this book, a lot of the pieces are worked in rounds instead of rows. You will see that one chain stitch is made at the end of each round. This chain stitch allows you to get your yarn high enough so you can begin the next round of stitches. You will not work any stitches into the chain itself.

How to make a slip knot:

1. Make a loop by crossing the working strand of yarn over the tail end of yarn.
2. Insert hook through the loop and pull the working strand back through the loop.
3. Pull both of the ends to tighten the slip knot around the hook.

How to make a chain stitch:

4. Slip knot is now on hook.
5. Yarn over hook.
6. Draw hooked yarn through loop on hook. Resist the urge to pull tightly after completing the stitch. You have now made one chain stitch.
7. This is what a chain stitch looks like at the end of each round.

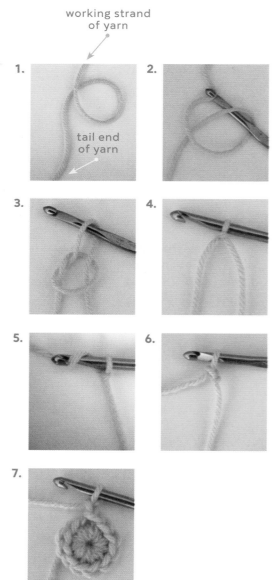

working strand of yarn

tail end of yarn

1.

2.

3.

4.

5.

6.

7.

SLIP STITCH (SL ST) JOIN

When the pattern says to join at the end of each round, that means you will make a slip stitch join. You will insert your hook into the first stitch, which is the first *single crochet* you made at the beginning of the round, not the chain 1. Slip stitch by pulling the working strand of yarn straight through the single crochet stitch and the loop on your hook. From here you will chain 1 and continue by following the pattern for the second round.

How to make a slip stitch join:

1. Insert hook through the top of the first stitch of the previous round.
2. Yarn over hook.
3. Draw hooked yarn straight through the stitch and the loop on hook. This is a slip stitch join completed after you've pulled the yarn through.

1.

2.

3.

> ### YARN COLOR CHANGES
>
> For certain patterns, such as Zina the Zebra, you'll need to change yarn colors. Don't be intimidated! The process is actually quite simple. When it's time to change colors of yarn, join in the new color by using your hook to pull the new-color yarn through the loops of your old color, leaving about 5 inches of yarn for the tail. Continue crocheting with the new color following the pattern.

SINGLE CROCHET (SC)

The single crochet is one of the most basic and easiest stitches. It is the stitch you will use most frequently when making your amigurumi animals. Master this stitch and you can make almost anything!

How to make a single crochet:

1. Insert hook into stitch and yarn over hook.
2. Draw yarn through stitch, so there are now 2 loops on the hook.
3. Yarn over hook.
4. Pull through both loops.

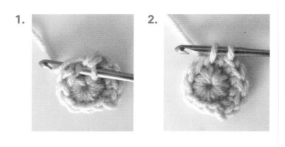

HALF DOUBLE CROCHET (HDC)

The half double crochet allows you to make a slightly taller stitch than the single crochet but not as tall as the double crochet. It sits nicely in between the two!

How to make a half double crochet:

1. Yarn over hook.
2. Insert hook into stitch and yarn over hook again.
3. Pull yarn through stitch so you now have 3 loops on your hook.
4. Yarn over hook again.
5. Pull through all 3 loops.

DOUBLE CROCHET (DC)

The double crochet is another common stitch and is twice as tall as the single crochet. It's not used as frequently in amigurumi, but there are a few places where this stitch is needed when working up these animals.

How to make a double crochet:

1. Yarn over hook.
2. Insert hook into stitch and yarn over hook again.
3. Draw yarn through stitch so you now have 3 loops on hook.
4. Yarn over hook and pull through the first 2 loops.
5. You now have 2 loops left on hook.
6. Yarn over hook.
7. Pull through remaining 2 loops.

1.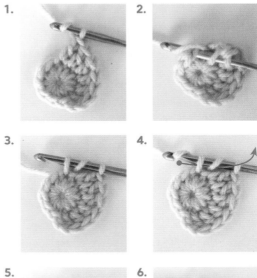

2.

3.

4.

5.

6.

7.

Special Stitches

There are a few special stitches that we should go over before diving into the patterns.

MAGIC RING

Many of the animal parts start with a *magic ring*. The magic ring allows you to begin your crochet over an adjustable loop so you can pull your starting round tight enough so that no hole is left.

How to make a magic ring:

1. Make a loop by crossing the working strand of yarn over the tail of the yarn. Insert hook through the loop but do not pull to tighten and instead leave the loop open. This loop is the magic ring.

2. Yarn over hook and pull through to make a chain 1. The chain 1 does not count as your first stitch.

3. Insert hook back through the magic ring, yarn over hook and pull the working strand of yarn through the loop again.

4. You now have 2 loops on the hook. Yarn over hook and pull the yarn through all the loops on the hook to complete your first single crochet, worked over the magic ring.

5. Continue to create as many stitches over the magic ring as stated in the pattern.

6. When finished, join to the first single crochet and pull the loop by the yarn tail to tighten and close the ring.

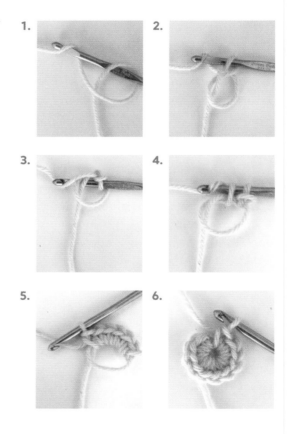

INCREASING AND DECREASING (2 SC AND SC2TOG)

Increase and decrease stitches are very important when making amigurumi. They are how the project takes shape.

An increase isn't labeled as any kind of special stitch, but you will encounter instructions such as "2 sc in first st," which is the increase. To work this, simply make two single crochets in one stitch.

A decrease, on the other hand, is a little trickier. To decrease, you will be working a single crochet decrease, abbreviated as sc2tog. You will basically crochet two stitches together in order to eliminate one stitch from the round.

How to make a single crochet increase (2 sc):
1. Make 2 single crochet stitches in the same stitch.
2. Both stitches sit together to make an increase (an extra stitch in round).

How to make a single crochet decrease (sc2tog):
1. Insert your hook into the first stitch. Yarn over hook and draw back through the stitch. Do not complete the stitch as normal.
2. Insert hook in the next stitch. Yarn over hook and draw through the stitch. There are now 3 loops on the hook.
3. Yarn over hook and draw through all 3 loops on the hook.
4. You have now crocheted 2 stitches into 1 and completed the single crochet decrease.

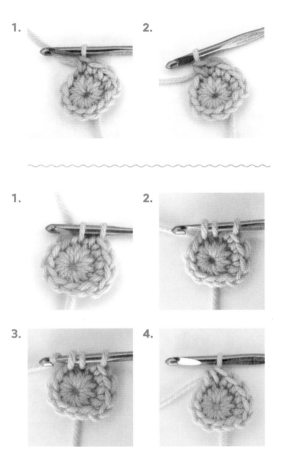

PART TWO

Finishing

Finishing your amigurumi consists of a few different techniques. In this section I will show you how to stuff your amigurumi, join the parts, close up the pieces, and add details to the face and body. This is the part that will bring your amigurumi to life! You will be able to finally see it come together and take on a personality. With a few tips and tricks, you can get your amigurumi to look its best with clean seams, perfect stuffing, and all the parts connected properly.

Stuffing Your Amigurumi

In concept, stuffing seems like the easy part. You just stuff the fiberfill into the crocheted pieces, right? Well in theory, yes, that is all there is to it, but there are two things that can go wrong: overstuffing and understuffing. You know you have overstuffed your animal if you can see the fiberfill start to poke through your stitches. Overstuffing will also cause the body parts to stick out funny or become lumpy and deformed. You need to keep in mind that the acrylic yarn has a lot of stretch to it and it will become misshapen if it is overly stuffed. Now, on the flip side, if you understuff, the animal will be limp and may not be able to sit on its own. It can also have the same side effects as overstuffing where the body parts may not look quite right because they haven't been filled enough.

So how do you get the perfect amount of stuffing into your amigurumi? The key is to stuff as you go. Little by little you will want to fill your piece or at least begin to stuff before you get to the decrease rounds of your pattern. Stuff enough in so that each part of your animal is well-formed yet still squishable. You should not be able to see the stuffing popping out of seams or between stitches. Use the stuffing to your advantage. This is your chance to mold and form your animal to look just the way you want it! As mentioned before, the yarn stretches and you can control the firmness. For instance, on Edward the Elephant you will want the trunk to be sturdy and to curve upward. Part of the curve will happen because of the way it is crocheted, but use the stuffing to help it have that nice curve. Stuff more in the top and less along the bend if needed. You will get a feel for it as you go.

Begin stuffing arms and legs when they are still short and you can easily begin filling the bottom with fiberfill.

Continue to stuff as you go. Approximately every 5 to 7 rounds of crochet you should add more stuffing.

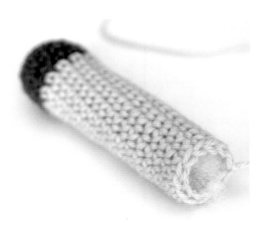

Finish stuffing and shaping your piece with fiberfill before attaching the crocheted amigurumi parts together.

Joining the Parts

Joining your amigurumi is a very important part of the process. This is also one of the most intimidating parts to conquer. When making these amigurumi animals you will have several parts that need to be attached together. Most of them will have an end that is open (an *open-ended piece*) with stuffing sticking out of it just waiting to be attached to a larger body piece (a *solid piece*). For instance, the snout of the bear that needs to be attached to the head. You want the connections of these pieces to look as neat and tidy as possible. The first thing to do is to make sure you leave a long tail when fastening off each part. If you cut the end too short, you won't have a yarn strand long enough to sew one body part to another.

JOINING THE PARTS TUTORIAL

1. Take the long yarn tail from your open-ended piece and thread it through your tapestry needle.
2. Hold the two pieces that need to be stitched together in place. Make sure that you have them lined up and placed exactly where you want them. Removing and repositioning after it's been sewn together is possible but can be frustrating and messy.
3. Insert the tapestry needle through a stitch in the solid piece.
4. Now bring the tapestry needle back through a stitch on the edge of your open-ended piece.
5. Continue to weave the tapestry needle in and out of stitches around the edge of your open-ended piece and through the solid piece until completely closed. If you need to stuff the piece a little more before sewing everything shut feel free to do so.

With your tapestry needle and long loose end of yarn, attach ear to head. Pinch ear closed and weave your needle through both the edge of the ear and the head stitches at the same time, also called a whip stitch. Arms should be stitched on the same way.

Work tapestry needle under the tops of the edge stitches. Notice how the needle slides under the tops of those single crochet stitches along the edge of each piece.

Weave needle in and out along the edge and through the head stitches at the same time. Legs should be stitched on the same way.

Hold in place and position while stitching your embellishments on. Be mindful of where you are placing your needle and go slow.

TIPS ABOUT PLACEMENT OF APPENDAGES

It's all about balance. Carefully place the legs so they are sticking out in a way so that your animal can sit up! In general with these patterns, this is about 7 rounds up from the bottom and 15 stitches apart.

To make the parts (like the head) less wobbly, you may want to make a second stitching lap around the place where you are attaching the head to the body with your tapestry needle.

Symmetry is important. Arms and ears should be placed evenly on either side of the head. Count rows and stitches to make sure you are attaching them in identical places.

The starting rounds of your piece will always have cleaner-looking stitches than your ending rounds. This is because the increase stitches make nice tight and clean rounds whereas the decrease stitches are trickier and tend to leave larger spaces between your stitches. As such, always attach the head to the location where you close the body. That way the neat beginning rounds are facing out for all to see. There are some exceptions to this, such as with the lamb and kangaroo patterns where your last rows actually become the nose.

Make sure the leg is facing the proper direction. "Toes" should be upward. Weave tapestry needle through the top of the leg opening stitches and the bottom of the body. If you attach the legs about 7 rows up from the body, your amigurumi should be able to sit upright.

Second leg should be placed in a mirrored position from the first. Use the rounds of stitches on the body to your advantage. Make sure you are stitching to the same spot as your first leg, just on the other side of the body.

Fastening & Closing Up

As I mentioned in the section about joining the parts, you will quickly notice that your decrease rounds look messier than your increase rounds. There are a few things you can do when closing your amigurumi parts to make them look their best!

When finishing the head or other parts that need to be completely closed, use your tapestry needle for the last round instead of your crochet hook. Sometimes it is difficult to get your crochet hook underneath the stitches when the rounds get small. Take your tapestry needle and weave it underneath the stitches in your final round and pull tight to close it.

Then when you weave in the tail, go back through and between stitches that seem spaced out to bring them together and try to close gaps.

It is also very important that you weave in your ends well so your amigurumi doesn't fall apart, unravel, or come undone. A good rule of thumb is to weave the ends in 3 times, going through the middle of the yarn fibers in opposing directions. Remember it is crucial to leave yourself enough yarn to weave in the ends properly! Don't cut those ends too short. There is also a small shortcut you can do with amigurumi: Feel free to tuck those long ends into the inside of your project. You will still need to weave them in, but no need to clip off or make sure they are super neat if they are going to be living on the inside of your project. Push the

Stuff body to desired firmness and continue to follow the pattern to decrease with your crochet hook. Safety eyes, nose, and most other face embellishments should already be added before closing. Ears and some other features will be attached later.

Sometimes it is difficult to use your hook on the last round to close your piece. You can use your tapestry needle to work under each stitch all the way around to close the head.

Pull tightly to ensure your piece is tightly closed. Weave in your ends so it doesn't come unraveled.

tapestry needle through the piece to the other side, pull the yarn through and cut it, and then watch it disappear!

Weaving in your ends means hiding your loose ends so they don't show on your finished piece, and, in doing so, making sure they are woven in securely so your amigurumi doesn't unravel or fall apart.

You will need to weave in your ends during several parts of the process.

First you will notice that where you started your magic ring and where you change color (like in many of the legs and arms) there will be loose ends to weave in. The nice thing about amigurumi is that a lot of the ends can be hidden inside the open-ended appendages. Secure the loose ends and then just leave them long and stuff them in with the fiberfill!

Weave your strands on the inside of the pieces with your tapestry needle a few times (no need to go overboard since they will be on the inside of your animal). Knot the loose ends if desired and leave the ends long. No need to clip the yarn strands short with scissors.

The other times you will need to weave in your ends is after you have joined the parts of the animal together and when you have finished closing a 3D piece (like the head). These loose ends will need to be woven in more carefully and neatly since they won't be hidden on the inside.

The method to weaving in your ends is pretty simple: With your tapestry needle, weave the strand into different stitches 3 to 5 times within the same color area as the yarn strand. You will want to make sure you don't weave your end in a straight line, otherwise there is a chance your project could come unraveled. So purposely weave from different angles and directions. Pull the yarn strand tightly and snip it with scissors close to your work. Be careful not to actually cut the stitches in your amigurumi piece.

Loose ends that can be secured and stuffed into animal leg.

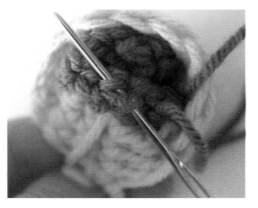

Weave like-color ends into like-color places on your project.

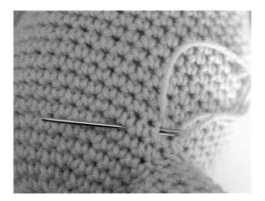

Ends will have to be woven in on the outside of your project when attaching limbs and closing 3D pieces.

Snip yarn end close to project after it is securely woven in. Be careful not to cut your crochet stitches!

FACE AND BODY DETAILS

Most of the animals featured in this book have pretty simple faces and minimal embellishments since this is geared toward beginner amigurumi crafters. A few times you will see that you need to use your tapestry needle to stitch on face elements like the whiskers on Callie the Cat, the mouth on Benny the Bear, and the nose and mouth on Lilly the Lamb. Take your time and be careful and intentional with your stitches. Once you have the safety eyes attached in the correct spots, you can use those as the centerpiece of the face and let the other parts of the face form around it.

It helps to stitch on any details (like the whiskers) before you stuff and close the head. This will allow more room for you to work and get the details just right. It will also allow space to weave in your ends. Don't be discouraged if you feel like you need to redo the details. It takes practice!

Take your tapestry needle and a long strand of yarn in the color needed for a specific detail. Stitch through the inside of the head and back through the front of the head. Use your stitches from the head as your guide and make purposeful placements. Embroider details in the shape shown for that particular animal. End with the needle poking through on the inside of your amigurumi and weave in your ends.

Make sure the location of the safety eye is exactly where you want it before attaching the washer to the back. You cannot move it once the washer is locked into place.

Press down firmly to attach the washer to the back of the safety eye. This goes on the inside of your amigurumi piece. When it makes a click you know it is locked into place.

The safety nose is similar to the safety eye, just bigger. Make sure you lock it in place and then stuff your piece. You won't be able to feel or see the backside of your safety nose or eyes once the amigurumi is stuffed and put together.

The nose should be placed with the point facing downward. It should be snug and secure.

PART THREE

Patterns A to Z

Each of the 26 animal amigurumi patterns in the book are written out from start to finish and have instructions within the pattern for how to assemble and finish each animal. You will notice that every single animal body and head begins with the exact same pattern! All of the body parts such as the legs, arms, ears, wings, and snouts also have a standard set of body parts. For instance, the bear, giraffe, unicorn, zebra, and yak all have the same snout. And the whale fins are the same pattern as the penguin and owl feet. I wanted to simplify the process by reusing basic shapes made with simple stitches, making these animals as easy as possible. The result is incredible! Upon first glance, you wouldn't be able to tell that most of the animals are crocheted from virtually the exact same pattern. It's amazing what can be created just by changing up the yarn color and a few embellishments. Each of the amigurumi are unique and will be slightly different sizes, but on average each of the amigurumi animals measures approximately 10 inches tall by 8 inches wide (from head to foot).

ALEX THE *Alligator*

Gentle and sweet and the perfect way to start out our alphabet animals! Alex the Alligator is wide-eyed and ready to be stitched up with love. Once you make this gator, you will want to make the rest of the A to Z critters!

Size: 10 inches tall x 8 inches wide

Materials:
- Bernat Super Value Yarn in Lush (dark green)
- Bernat Super Value Yarn in Soft Fern (light green)
- Bernat Super Value Yarn in White (just a small amount for the eyes)
- Size H Crochet Hook
- 12mm Safety Eyes
- Poly-fil Fiber Stuffing
- Tapestry Needle

Body:

With Lush yarn, create a magic ring, ch 1 and make 10 sc in ring, join to first sc, ch 1.

Round 2: 2 sc in each st around, join, ch 1. (20 sts)

Round 3: *2 sc in next st, sc in next st, repeat from * around, join, ch 1. (30 sts)

Round 4: Sc in each st around, join, ch 1.

Round 5: *2 sc in next st, sc in next 2 sts, repeat from * around, join, ch 1. (40 sts)

Round 6: Sc in each st around, join, ch 1.

Round 7: *2 sc in next st, sc in next 3 sts, repeat from * around, join, ch 1. (50 sts)

Rounds 8–19: Sc in each st around, join, ch 1.

Round 20: *Sc2tog, sc in next 3 sts, repeat from * around, join, ch 1. (40 sts)

Rounds 21–22: Sc in each st around, join, ch 1.

Round 23: *Sc2tog, sc in next 2 sts, repeat from * around, join, ch 1. (30 sts)

Rounds 24–25: Sc in each st around, join, ch 1.

Round 26: *Sc2tog, sc in next st, repeat from * around, join, ch 1. (20 sts)

Rounds 27–28: Sc in each st around, join, ch 1.

Round 29: Sc2tog around, join. (10 sts)

Fasten off leaving a long tail and stuff, leaving top open.

Head:

With Lush yarn, create a magic ring, ch 1 and make 10 sc in ring, join to first sc, ch 1.

Round 2: 2 sc in each st around, join, ch 1. (20 sts)

Round 3: Sc in each st around, join, ch 1.

Round 4: *2 sc in next st, sc in next st, repeat from * around, join, ch 1. (30 sts)

Round 5: Sc in each st around, join, ch 1.

Round 6: *2 sc in next st, sc in next 2 sts, repeat from * around, join, ch 1. (40 sts)

Round 7: *2 sc in next st, sc in next 3 sts, repeat from * around, join, ch 1. (50 sts)

Rounds 8–15: Sc in each st around, join, ch 1.

Round 16: *Sc2tog, sc in next 3 sts, repeat from * around, join, ch 1. (40 sts)

Round 17: Sc in each st around, join, ch 1.

Round 18: *Sc2tog, sc in next 2 sts, repeat from * around, join, ch 1. (30 sts)

Round 19: Sc in each st around, join, ch 1.

Round 20: *Sc2tog, sc in next st, repeat from * around, join, ch 1. (20 sts)

Round 21: Sc in each st around, join, ch 1.

Stuff before closing the head.

Round 22: Sc2tog around, join, ch 1. (10 sts)

Round 23: Sc2tog around, join. (5 sts)

Fasten off leaving a long tail.

Use long tail to close final round and weave in ends.

Use long tail of body to sew on head.

Legs (make 2):

With Lush yarn, create a magic ring, ch 1 and make 6 sc in ring, join to first sc, ch 1.

Round 2: 2 sc in each st around, join, ch 2. (12 sts)

Round 3: 2 dc in next 3 sts, 2 hdc in next 2 sts, 2 sc in next 5 sts, 2 hdc in last 2 sts, join, ch 1. (24 sts)

Round 4: Working in back loops only for this round, sc in each st around, join, ch 1.

Rounds 5–6: Sc in each st around, join, ch 1.

Round 7: Sc2tog 6 times, sc in remaining 12 sts, join, ch 1. (18 sts)

Round 8: Sc in each st around, join, ch 1.

Round 9: Sc2tog 5 times, sc in remaining 8 sts, join, ch 1. (13 sts)

Rounds 10–14: Sc in each st around, join, ch 1.

Fasten off leaving a long tail and stuff.

Use long tail to sew onto bottom of body.

Arms (make 2):

With Lush yarn, create a magic ring, ch 1 and make 10 sc in ring, join to first sc, ch 1.

Round 2: *2 sc in next st, sc in next st, repeat from * around, join, ch 1. (15 sts)

Rounds 3–4: Sc in each st around, join, ch 1.

Round 5: *Sc2tog, sc in next 3 sts, repeat from * around, join, ch 1. (12 sts)

Rounds 6–22: Sc in each st around, join, ch 1.

Fasten off leaving a long tail and stuff.

Flatten opening and use long tail to sew onto body under the head.

Belly:

With Soft Fern yarn, ch 11, sc in second ch from hook and next 9 chs, ch 1, turn.

Row 2: 2 sc in next st, sc in next 8 sts, 2 sc in last st, ch 1, turn. (12 sts)

Rows 3–6: Sc in each st across, ch 1, turn.

Row 7: Sc2tog, sc in next 8 sts, sc2tog over last 2 sts, ch 1, turn. (10 sts)

Row 8: Sc in each st across, ch 1, turn.

Row 9: Sc2tog, sc in next 6 sts, sc2tog over last 2 sts, ch 1, turn. (8 sts)

Rows 10–13: Sc in each st across, ch 1, turn.

Row 14: Sc2tog, sc in next 4 sts, sc2tog over last 2 sts, ch 1, turn. (6 sts)

Row 15: Sc2tog, sc in next 2 sts, sc2tog over last 2 sts, ch 1, turn. (4 sts)

Row 16: Sc2tog twice. (2 sts)

Fasten off leaving a long tail and sew onto belly area of body.

Tail:

With Lush yarn, create a magic ring, ch 1 and make 4 sc in ring, join to first sc, ch 1.

Round 2: *2 sc in next st, sc in next st, repeat from * around, join, ch 1. (6 sts)

Round 3: Sc in each st around, join, ch 1.

Round 4: *2 sc in next st, sc in next 2 sts, repeat from * around, join, ch 1. (8 sts)

Round 5: Sc in each st around, join, ch 1.

Round 6: *2 sc in next st, sc in next 3 sts, repeat from * around, join, ch 1. (10 sts)

Round 7: Sc in each st around, join, ch 1.

Round 8: *2 sc in next st, sc in next 4 sts, repeat from * around, join, ch 1. (12 sts)

Round 9: Sc in each st around, join, ch 1.

Round 10: *2 sc in next st, sc in next 5 sts, repeat from * around, join, ch 1. (14 sts)

Round 11: Sc in each st around, join, ch 1.

Round 12: *2 sc in next st, sc in next 6 sts, repeat from * around, join, ch 1. (16 sts)

Round 13: Sc in each st around, join, ch 1.

Round 14: *2 sc in next st, sc in next 7 sts, repeat from * around, join, ch 1. (18 sts)

Round 15: Sc in each st around, join, ch 1.

Round 16: *2 sc in next st, sc in next 8 sts, repeat from * around, join, ch 1. (20 sts)

Round 17: *2 sc in next st, sc in next 9 sts, repeat from * around, join, ch 1. (22 sts)

Round 18: *2 sc in next st, sc in next 10 sts, repeat from * around, join. (24 sts)

Fasten off leaving a long tail and stuff.

Use long tail to sew onto back bottom of body.

Snout:

With Lush yarn, ch 11, sc in second ch from hook and next 8 chs, 3 sc in last ch.

Now working on other side of starting ch, sc in first 9 chs, 3 sc in last ch, join to first sc, ch 1. (24 sts)

Round 2: Sc in first 9 sts, 2 sc in next 3 sts, sc in next 9 sts, 2 sc in last 3 sts, join to first sc, ch 1. (30 sts)

Rounds 3–12: Sc in each st around, join, ch 1.

Fasten off leaving a long tail and stuff.

Use long tail to sew onto head.

Nostrils (make 2):

With Lush yarn, create a magic ring, ch 1 and make 6 sc in ring, do not join.

Fasten off leaving a long tail and sew nostrils onto top of snout.

Eyes (make 2):

Back Part of Eye (make 2):

With Lush yarn, create a magic ring, ch 1 and make 8 hdc in ring, join to first hdc, ch 1.

Round 2: 2 hdc in each st around, join. (16 hdc)

Fasten off leaving a long tail.

Front Part of Eye (make 2):

With White yarn, create a magic ring, ch 1 and make 8 hdc in ring, join to first hdc.

Fasten off leaving a long tail.

Secure safety eyes into center of white eyeball.

Use long tail to sew white front part of eye to green back part of eye (the green part of eye should automatically curl around the white).

Use long tail of back part of eye to sew onto head, resting above the snout.

BENNY THE *Bear*

Get big bear hugs from Benny! He is fully customizable with any color combo you can think of. He makes for a great gift and fun project!

Size: 10 inches tall x 8 inches wide

Materials:
- Bernat Super Value Yarn in Honey (dark brown)
- Bernat Super Value Yarn in Oatmeal (light brown)
- Size H Crochet Hook
- 12mm Safety Eyes
- 18mm Safety Nose
- Poly-fil Fiber Stuffing
- Tapestry Needle

Body:

With Honey yarn, create a magic ring, ch 1 and make 10 sc in ring, join to first sc, ch 1.

Round 2: 2 sc in each st around, join, ch 1. (20 sts)

Round 3: *2 sc in next st, sc in next st, repeat from * around, join, ch 1. (30 sts)

Round 4: Sc in each st around, join, ch 1.

Round 5: *2 sc in next st, sc in next 2 sts, repeat from * around, join, ch 1. (40 sts)

Round 6: Sc in each st around, join, ch 1.

Round 7: 2 sc in next st, sc in next 3 sts, repeat from * around, join, ch 1. (50 sts)

Rounds 8–19: Sc in each st around, join, ch 1.

Round 20: *Sc2tog, sc in next 3 sts, repeat from * around, join, ch 1. (40 sts)

Rounds 21–22: Sc in each st around, join, ch 1.

Round 23: *Sc2tog, sc in next 2 sts, repeat from * around, join, ch 1. (30 sts)

Rounds 24–25: Sc in each st around, join, ch 1.

Round 26: *Sc2tog, sc in next st, repeat from * around, join, ch 1. (20 sts)

Rounds 27–28: Sc in each st around, join, ch 1.

Round 29: Sc2tog around, join. (10 sts)

Fasten off leaving a long tail and stuff, leaving top open.

Head:

With Honey yarn, create a magic ring, ch 1 and make 10 sc in ring, join to first sc, ch 1.

Round 2: 2 sc in each st around, join, ch 1. (20 sts)

Round 3: Sc in each st around, join, ch 1.

Round 4: *2 sc in next st, sc in next st, repeat from * around, join, ch 1. (30 sts)

Round 5: Sc in each st around, join, ch 1.

Round 6: *2 sc in next st, sc in next 2 sts, repeat from * around, join, ch 1. (40 sts)

Round 7: *2 sc in next st, sc in next 3 sts, repeat from * around, join, ch 1. (50 sts)

Rounds 8–15: Sc in each st around, join, ch 1.

Round 16: *Sc2tog, sc in next 3 sts, repeat from * around, join, ch 1. (40 sts)

Round 17: Sc in each st around, join, ch 1.

Round 18: *Sc2tog, sc in next 2 sts, repeat from * around, join, ch 1. (30 sts)

Round 19: Sc in each st around, join, ch 1.

Round 20: *Sc2tog, sc in next st, repeat from * around, join, ch 1. (20 sts)

Round 21: Sc in each st around, join, ch 1.

At this point attach the safety eyes. Then stuff before closing the head.

Round 22: Sc2tog around, join, ch 1. (10 sts)

Round 23: Sc2tog around, join. (5 sts)

Fasten off leaving a long tail.

Use long tail to close final round and weave in ends.

Use long tail of body to sew on head.

Legs (make 2):

With Oatmeal yarn, create a magic ring, ch 1 and make 6 sc in ring, join to first sc, ch 1.

Round 2: 2 sc in each st around, join, ch 2. (12 sts)

Round 3: 2 dc in first 3 sts, 2 hdc in next 2 sts, 2 sc in next 5 sts, 2 hdc in last 2 sts, join, ch 1. (24 sts)

Round 4: Working in back loops only for this round, sc in each st around, join, *change to Honey yarn*, ch 1.

Rounds 5–6: Sc in each st around, join, ch 1.

Round 7: Sc2tog 6 times, sc in remaining 12 sts, join, ch 1. (18 sts)

Round 8: Sc in each st around, join, ch 1.

Round 9: Sc2tog 5 times, sc in remaining 8 sts, join, ch 1. (13 sts)

Rounds 10–14: Sc in each st around, join, ch 1.

Fasten off leaving a long tail and stuff.

Use long tail to sew onto bottom of body.

Arms (make 2):

With Honey yarn, create a magic ring, ch 1 and make 10 sc in ring, join to first sc, ch 1.

Round 2: *2 sc in next st, sc in next st, repeat from * around, join, ch 1. (15 sts)

Rounds 3–4: Sc in each st around, join, ch 1.

Round 5: *Sc2tog, sc in next 3 sts, repeat from * around, join, ch 1. (12 sts)

Rounds 6–22: Sc in each st around, join, ch 1.

Fasten off leaving a long tail and stuff.

Flatten opening and use long tail to sew onto body under the head.

Ears (make 2):

Outer Ear (make 2):

With Honey yarn, create a magic ring, ch 1 and make 8 sc in ring, join to first sc, ch 1.

Round 2: 2 sc in each st around, join, ch 1. (16 sts)

Round 3: *2 sc in next st, sc in next 3 sts, repeat from * around, join, ch 1. (20 sts)

Rounds 4–7: Sc in each st around, join, ch 1.

Round 8: *Sc2tog, sc in next 3 sts, repeat from * around, join. (16 sts)

Fasten off leaving a long tail.

Inner Ear (make 2):

With Oatmeal yarn, create a magic ring, ch 1 and make 6 sc in ring, join to first sc, ch 1.

Round 2: *2 sc in next st, sc in next st, repeat from * around, join. (9 sts)

Fasten off leaving a long tail.

Use long tail to sew inner ear onto the front side
of outer ear.

No need to stuff outer ear.

Use long tail of outer ear to sew ears onto top
of head.

Snout:

With Oatmeal yarn, create a magic ring, ch 1 and
make 10 sc in ring, join to first sc, ch 1.

Round 2: 2 sc in each st around, join, ch 1. (20 sts)

Round 3: Sc in each st around, join, ch 1.

Round 4: *2 sc in next st, sc in next st, repeat from *
around, join, ch 1. (30 sts)

Rounds 5–7: Sc in each st around, join, ch 1.

Fasten off leaving a long tail.

Add safety nose and sew on a little smile using
Oatmeal yarn before stuffing.

Use long tail to sew onto head.

CALLIE THE *Cat*

Meet Callie! This purrfectly plush kitty is ready to curl up and cuddle. Cat lovers everywhere will want to stitch up this cute cat. Minimal embellishments make this one of the easier projects and the color possibilities are endless!

Size: 10 inches tall x 8 inches wide

Materials:
- Bernat Super Value Yarn in Soft Gray
- Bernat Super Value Yarn in White
- Size H Crochet Hook
- 12mm Safety Eyes
- 18mm Safety Nose
- Poly-fil Fiber Stuffing
- Tapestry Needle

Body:

With Soft Gray yarn, create a magic ring, ch 1 and make 10 sc in ring, join to first sc, ch 1.

Round 2: 2 sc in each st around, join, ch 1. (20 sts)

Round 3: *2 sc in next st, sc in next st, repeat from * around, join, ch 1. (30 sts)

Round 4: Sc in each st around, join, ch 1.

Round 5: *2 sc in next st, sc in next 2 sts, repeat from * around, join, ch 1. (40 sts)

Round 6: Sc in each st around, join, ch 1.

Round 7: *2 sc in next st, sc in next 3 sts, repeat from * around, join, ch 1. (50 sts)

Rounds 8–19: Sc in each st around, join, ch 1.

Round 20: *Sc2tog, sc in next 3 sts, repeat from * around, join, ch 1. (40 sts)

Rounds 21–22: Sc in each st around, join, ch 1.

Round 23: *Sc2tog, sc in next 2 sts, repeat from * around, join, ch 1. (30 sts)

Rounds 24–25: Sc in each st around, join, ch 1.

Round 26: *Sc2tog, sc in next st, repeat from * around, join, ch 1. (20 sts)

Rounds 27–28: Sc in each st around, join, ch 1.

Round 29: Sc2tog around, join. (10 sts)

Fasten off leaving a long tail and stuff, leaving top open.

Head:

With Soft Gray yarn, create a magic ring, ch 1 and make 10 sc in ring, join to first sc, ch 1.

Round 2: 2 sc in each st around, join, ch 1. (20 sts)

Round 3: Sc in each st around, join, ch 1.

Round 4: *2 sc in next st, sc in next st, repeat from * around, join, ch 1. (30 sts)

Round 5: Sc in each st around, join, ch 1.

Round 6: *2 sc in next st, sc in next 2 sts, repeat from * around, join, ch 1. (40 sts)

Round 7: *2 sc in next st, sc in next 3 sts, repeat from * around, join, ch 1. (50 sts)

Rounds 8–15: Sc in each st around, join, ch 1.

Round 16: *Sc2tog, sc in next 3 sts, repeat from * around, join, ch 1. (40 sts)

Round 17: Sc in each st around, join, ch 1.

Round 18: *Sc2tog, sc in next 2 sts, repeat from * around, join, ch 1. (30 sts)

Round 19: Sc in each st around, join, ch 1.

Round 20: *Sc2tog, sc in next st, repeat from * around, join, ch 1. (20 sts)

Round 21: Sc in each st around, join, ch 1.

At this point attach the safety eyes (about 12 rounds up) and nose (about 11 rounds up). Sew on two strands of White yarn for the whiskers on either side of the nose. Then stuff before closing the head.

Round 22: Sc2tog around, join, ch 1. (10 sts)

Round 23: Sc2tog around, join. (5 sts)

Fasten off leaving a long tail.

Use long tail to close final round and weave in ends.

Use long tail of body to sew on head.

Legs (make 2):

With White yarn, create a magic ring, ch 1 and make 6 sc in ring, join to first sc, ch 1.

Round 2: 2 sc in each st around, join, ch 2. (12 sts)

Round 3: 2 dc in first 3 sts, 2 hdc in next 2 sts, 2 sc in next 5 sts, 2 hdc in last 2 sts, join, ch 1. (24 sts)

Round 4: Working in back loops only for this round, sc in each st around, join, *change to Soft Gray yarn*, ch 1.

Rounds 5–6: Sc in each st around, join, ch 1.

Round 7: Sc2tog 6 times, sc in remaining 12 sts, join, ch 1. (18 sts)

Round 8: Sc in each st around, join, ch 1.

Round 9: Sc2tog 5 times, sc in remaining 8 sts, join, ch 1. (13 sts)

Rounds 10–14: Sc in each st around, join, ch 1.

Fasten off leaving a long tail and stuff.

Use long tail to sew onto bottom of body.

Arms (make 2):

With White yarn, create a magic ring, ch 1 and make 10 sc in ring, join to first sc, ch 1.

Round 2: *2 sc in next st, sc in next st, repeat from * around, join, ch 1. (15 sts)

Rounds 3–4: Sc in each st around, join, ch 1.

Round 5: *Sc2tog, sc in next 3 sts, repeat from * around, join, *change to Soft Gray yarn*, ch 1. (12 sts)

Rounds 6–22: Sc in each st around, join, ch 1.

Fasten off leaving a long tail and stuff.

Flatten opening and use long tail to sew onto body under the head.

Ears (make 2):

With Soft Gray yarn, create a magic ring, ch 1 and make 4 sc in ring, join to first sc, ch 1.

Round 2: Sc in each st around, join, ch 1.

Round 3: 2 sc in each st around, join, ch 1. (8 sts)

Round 4: Sc in each st around, join, ch 1.

Round 5: *2 sc in next st, sc in next st, repeat from * around, join, ch 1. (12 sts)

Round 6: Sc in each st around, join, ch 1.

Round 7: *2 sc in next st, sc in next 2 sts, repeat from * around, join, ch 1. (16 sts)

Rounds 8–9: Sc in each st around, join, ch 1.

Fasten off leaving a long tail. No need to stuff.

Use long tail to sew onto top sides of head.

Tail:

With Soft Gray yarn, create a magic ring, ch 1 and
    make 6 sc in ring, join to first sc, ch 1.

Round 2: Sc in each st around, join, ch 1.

Round 3: *2 sc in next st, sc in next st, repeat from *
    around, ch 1, turn. (9 sts)

Rounds 4–14: Sc in each st around, join, ch 1.

Fasten off leaving a long tail and stuff.

Use long tail to sew to bottom back of body.

DASH THE *Dog*

Dash the Dog is the most playful pup around! He loves squishy hugs and lots of snuggles. His big floppy ears make him a listener and he will sit upright next to you, making him a great companion! Stitch up this pup with two colors of worsted weight yarn and lots of love.

Size: 10 inches tall x 8 inches wide

Materials:
- Bernat Super Value Yarn in Oatmeal (light brown)
- Bernat Super Value Yarn in Taupe (dark brown)
- Size H Crochet Hook
- 12mm Safety Eyes
- 18mm Safety Nose
- Poly-fil Fiber Stuffing
- Tapestry Needle

Body:

With Oatmeal yarn, create a magic ring, ch 1 and make 10 sc in ring, join to first sc, ch 1.

Round 2: 2 sc in each st around, join, ch 1. (20 sts)

Round 3: *2 sc in next st, sc in next st, repeat from * around, join, ch 1. (30 sts)

Round 4: Sc in each st around, join, ch 1.

Round 5: *2 sc in next st, sc in next 2 sts, repeat from * around, join, ch 1. (40 sts)

Round 6: Sc in each st around, join, ch 1.

Round 7: *2 sc in next st, sc in next 3 sts, repeat from * around, join, ch 1. (50 sts)

Rounds 8–19: Sc in each st around, join, ch 1.

Round 20: *Sc2tog, sc in next 3 sts, repeat from * around, join, ch 1. (40 sts)

Rounds 21–22: Sc in each st around, join, ch 1.

Round 23: *Sc2tog, sc in next 2 sts, repeat from * around, join, ch 1. (30 sts)

Rounds 24–25: Sc in each st around, join, ch 1.

Round 26: *Sc2tog, sc in next st, repeat from * around, join, ch 1. (20 sts)

Rounds 27–28: Sc in each st around, join, ch 1.

Round 29: Sc2tog around, join. (10 sts)

Fasten off leaving a long tail and stuff, leaving top open.

Snout:

With Oatmeal yarn, ch 5, sc in second ch from hook and next 2 chs, 3 sc in last ch.

Now working on other side of ch, sc in first 3 chs, 3 sc in last ch, join, ch 1. (12 sts)

Round 2: Sc in first 3 sts, 2 sc in next 3 sts, sc in next 3 sts, 2 sc in last 3 sts, join, ch 1. (18 sts)

Rounds 3–4: Sc in each st around, join, ch 1.

Fasten off leaving a long tail.

Add safety nose toward the middle top of snout.

Eye Patch:

With Taupe yarn, create a magic ring, ch 1 and make 6 sc in ring, pull tight, do not join, ch 1, turn.

Row 2: 2 sc in first st, sc in next 4 sts, 2 sc in last st, ch 1, turn (8 sts).

Row 3: Sc in each st.

Fasten off leaving a long tail.

Place one of the safety eyes in the middle of eye patch and secure.

Head:

With Oatmeal yarn, create a magic ring, ch 1 and make 10 sc in ring, join to first sc, ch 1.

Round 2: 2 sc in each st around, join, ch 1. (20 sts)

Round 3: Sc in each st around, join, ch 1.

Round 4: *2 sc in next st, sc in next st, repeat from * around, join, ch 1. (30 sts)

Round 5: Sc in each st around, join, ch 1.

Round 6: *2 sc in next st, sc in next 2 sts, repeat from * around, join, ch 1. (40 sts)

Round 7: *2 sc in next st, sc in next 3 sts, repeat from * around, join, ch 1. (50 sts)

Rounds 8–15: Sc in each st around, join, ch 1.

Round 16: *Sc2tog, sc in next 3 sts, repeat from * around, join, ch 1. (40 sts)

Round 17: Sc in each st around, join, ch 1.

Round 18: *Sc2tog, sc in next 2 sts, repeat from * around, join, ch 1. (30 sts)

Round 19: Sc in each st around, join, ch 1.

Round 20: *Sc2tog, sc in next st, repeat from * around, join, ch 1. (20 sts)

Round 21: Sc in each st around, join, ch 1.

At this point sew on the snout and eye patch above the snout on the left-hand side and add remaining safety eye parallel to the first. Then stuff before closing the head.

Round 22: Sc2tog around, join, ch 1. (10 sts)

Round 23: Sc2tog around, join. (5 sts)

Fasten off and weave in ends.

Use long tail of body to sew on head.

Legs (make 2):

With Taupe yarn, create a magic ring, ch 1 and make 6 sc in ring, join to first sc, ch 1.

Round 2: 2 sc in each st around, join, ch 2. (12 sts)

Round 3: 2 dc in first 3 sts, 2 hdc in next 2 sts, 2 sc in next 5 sts, 2 hdc in last 2 sts, join, ch 1. (24 sts)

Round 4: Working in back loops only for this round, sc in each st around, join, *change to Oatmeal yarn*, ch 1.

Rounds 5–6: Sc in each st around, join, ch 1.

Round 7: Sc2tog 6 times, sc in remaining 12 sts, join, ch 1. (18 sts)

Round 8: Sc in each st around, join, ch 1.

Round 9: Sc2tog 5 times, sc in remaining 8 sts, join, ch 1. (13 sts)

Rounds 10–14: Sc in each st around, join, ch 1.

Fasten off leaving a long tail and stuff.

Use long tail to sew onto bottom of body.

Arms (make 2):

With Taupe yarn, create a magic ring, ch 1 and make 10 sc in ring, join to first sc, ch 1.

Round 2: *2 sc in next st, sc in next st, repeat from * around, join, ch 1. (15 sts)

Rounds 3–4: Sc in each st around, join, ch 1.

Round 5: *Sc2tog, sc in next 3 sts, repeat from * around, join, *change to Oatmeal yarn*, ch 1. (12 sts)

Rounds 6–22: Sc in each st around, join, ch 1.

Fasten off leaving a long tail and stuff.

Flatten opening and use long tail to sew onto body under the head.

Ears (make 2—one in each yarn color):

Create a magic ring, ch 1 and make 8 sc in ring, join to first sc, ch 1.

Round 2: 2 sc in each st around, join, ch 1. (16 sts)

Round 3: *2 sc in next st, sc in next 3 sts, repeat from * around, join, ch 1. (20 sts)

Rounds 4–8: Sc in each st around, join, ch 1.

Round 9: *Sc2tog, sc in next 3 sts, repeat from * around, join, ch 1. (16 sts)

Round 10: Sc in each st around, join, ch 1.

Round 11: *Sc2tog, sc in next 2 sts, repeat from * around, join, ch 1. (12 sts)

Rounds 12–19: Sc in each st around, join, ch 1.

Fasten off leaving a long tail. No need to stuff ears.

Use long tail to sew onto head about 3 or 4 rounds down from top.

Tail:

With Taupe yarn, create a magic ring, ch 1 and make 4 sc in ring, join, ch 1.

Round 2: Sc in each st around, join, ch 1.

Round 3: *2 sc in next st, sc in next st, repeat from * around, join, ch 1. (6 sts)

Round 4: Sc in each st around, join, ch 1.

Round 5: *2 sc in next st, sc in next 2 sts, repeat from * around, join, ch 1. (8 sts)

Round 6: Sc in each st around, join, ch 1.

Round 7: Sc2tog, sc in last 6 sts, join, ch 1. (7 sts)

Round 8: Sc in each st around, join, ch 1.

Round 9: Sc2tog, sc in last 5 sts, join. (6 sts)

Fasten off leaving a long tail and stuff lightly.

Use long tail to sew onto back of body.

EDWARD THE *Elephant*

One color is all you need to crochet Edward the Elephant. Big floppy ears and a curved trunk make this plush amigurumi irresistible! Edward is the perfect gender-neutral baby gift.

Size: 10 inches tall x 8 inches wide

Materials:
- Bernat Super Value Yarn in Sky
- Size H Crochet Hook
- 12mm Safety Eyes
- Poly-fil Fiber Stuffing
- Tapestry Needle
- Removable Stitch Marker (optional)

Body:

Create a magic ring, ch 1 and make 10 sc in ring, join to first sc, ch 1.

Round 2: 2 sc in each st around, join, ch 1. (20 sts)

Round 3: *2 sc in next st, sc in next st, repeat from * around, join, ch 1. (30 sts)

Round 4: Sc in each st around, join, ch 1.

Round 5: *2 sc in next st, sc in next 2 sts, repeat from * around, join, ch 1. (40 sts)

Round 6: Sc in each st around, join, ch 1.

Round 7: *2 sc in next st, sc in next 3 sts, repeat from * around, join, ch 1. (50 sts)

Rounds 8–19: Sc in each st around, join, ch 1.

Round 20: *Sc2tog, sc in next 3 sts, repeat from * around, join, ch 1. (40 sts)

Rounds 21–22: Sc in each st around, join, ch 1.

Round 23: *Sc2tog, sc in next 2 sts, repeat from * around, join, ch 1. (30 sts)

Rounds 24–25: Sc in each st around, join, ch 1.

Round 26: *Sc2tog, sc in next st, repeat from * around, join, ch 1. (20 sts)

Rounds 27–28: Sc in each st around, join, ch 1.

Round 29: Sc2tog around, join. (10 sts)

Fasten off leaving a long tail and stuff, leaving top open.

Head:

Create a magic ring, ch 1 and make 10 sc in ring, join to first sc, ch 1.

Round 2: 2 sc in each st around, join, ch 1. (20 sts)

Round 3: Sc in each st around, join, ch 1.

Round 4: *2 sc in next st, sc in next st, repeat from * around, join, ch 1. (30 sts)

Round 5: Sc in each st around, join, ch 1.

Round 6: *2 sc in next st, sc in next 2 sts, repeat from * around, join, ch 1. (40 sts)

Round 7: *2 sc in next st, sc in next 3 sts, repeat from * around, join, ch 1. (50 sts)

Rounds 8–15: Sc in each st around, join, ch 1.

Round 16: *Sc2tog, sc in next 3 sts, repeat from * around, join, ch 1. (40 sts)

Round 17: Sc in each st around, join, ch 1.

Round 18: *Sc2tog, sc in next 2 sts, repeat from * around, join, ch 1. (30 sts)

Round 19: Sc in each st around, join, ch 1.

Round 20: *Sc2tog, sc in next st, repeat from * around, join, ch 1. (20 sts)

Round 21: Sc in each st around, join, ch 1.

At this point attach the safety eyes between round 9 and 10 (about 5 sts apart). Then stuff before closing the head.

Round 22: Sc2tog around, join, ch 1. (10 sts)

Round 23: Sc2tog around, join. (5 sts)

Fasten off leaving a long tail.

Use long tail to close final round and weave in ends.

Use long tail of body to sew on head.

Legs (make 2):

Create a magic ring, ch 1 and make 6 sc in ring, join to first sc, ch 1.

Round 2: 2 sc in each st around, join, ch 2. (12 sts)

Round 3: 2 dc in first 3 sts, 2 hdc in next 2 sts, 2 sc in next 5 sts, 2 hdc in last 2 sts, join, ch 1. (24 sts)

Round 4: Working in back loops only for this round, sc in each st around, join, ch 1.

Rounds 5–6: Sc in each st around, join, ch 1.

Round 7: Sc2tog 6 times, sc in remaining 12 sts, join, ch 1. (18 sts)

Round 8: Sc in each st around, join, ch 1.

Round 9: Sc2tog 5 times, sc in remaining 8 sts, join, ch 1. (13 sts)

Rounds 10–14: Sc in each st around, join, ch 1.

Fasten off leaving a long tail and stuff.

Use long tail to sew onto bottom of body.

Arms (make 2):

Create a magic ring, ch 1 and make 10 sc in ring, join to first sc, ch 1.

Round 2: *2 sc in next st, sc in next st, repeat from * around, join, ch 1. (15 sts)

Rounds 3–4: Sc in each st around, join, ch 1.

Round 5: *Sc2tog, sc in next 3 sts, repeat from * around, join, ch 1. (12 sts)

Rounds 6–22: Sc in each st around, join, ch 1.

Fasten off leaving a long tail and stuff.

Flatten opening and use long tail to sew onto body under the head.

Trunk:

Create a magic ring, ch 1 and make 10 sc in ring, join to first sc. Continue to work in spiral form without joining or ch 1 until indicated. Use a removable stitch marker to indicate beginning of round if needed.

Round 2: Working in back loops only for this round, sc in each st around.

Rounds 3–5: Sc in each st around.

Round 6: Sc2tog, 2 sc in next st, sc in next 3 sts, 2 sc in next st, sc in next 3 sts. (11 sts)

Round 7: Sc2tog, sc in next 9 sts. (10 sts)

Round 8: Sc2tog, sc in next 4 sts, 2 sc in next st, sc in next 3 sts. (10 sts)

Round 9: 2 sc in next st, sc in next 4 sts, 2 sc in next st, sc in next 4 sts. (12 sts)

Round 10: Sc in each st around.

Round 11: *2 sc in next st, sc in next 3 sts, repeat from * around. (15 sts)

Rounds 12–13: Sc in each st around.

Round 14: Sc2tog, sc in next 3 st, 2 sc in next st, sc in next 3 sts, 2 sc in next st, sc in next 3 sts, sc2tog over last 2 sts, join, ch 1. (15 sts)

Round 15: Sc in first 6 sts, 2 sc in next 3 sts, sc in last 6 sts, join, ch 1. (18 sts)

Round 16: Sc in each st around, join.

Fasten off leaving a long tail.

Stuff trunk so it curves upward and use long tail to sew onto middle-front of head right below the eyes.

Ears (make 2):

Bigger Part of Ear (make 2):

Create a magic ring, ch 1 and make 10 sc in ring, join to first sc, ch 1.

Round 2: 2 sc in each st around, join, ch 1. (20 sts)

Round 3: Sc in each st around, join, ch 1.

Round 4: *2 sc in next st, sc in next st, repeat from * around, join, ch 1. (30 sts)

Rounds 5–10: Sc in each st around, join, ch 1.

Round 11: *Sc2tog, repeat from * around, join, ch 1. (15 sts)

Round 12: Sc in each st around, join, ch 1.

Round 13: Sc2tog around to last st, sc in last st, join. (8 sts)

Fasten off leaving a long tail.

Do not stuff.

Smaller Part of Ear (make 2):

Create a magic ring, ch 1 and make 10 sc in ring, join to first sc, ch 1.

Round 2: *2 sc in next st, sc in next st, repeat from * around, join, ch 1. (15 sts)

Rounds 3–5: Sc in each st around, join, ch 1.

Round 6: *Sc2tog, sc in next st, repeat from * around, join, ch 1. (10 sts)

Round 7: Sc in each st around, join.

Fasten off leaving a long tail.

Do not stuff.

With the bigger part of the ear on top and the smaller part of the ear on the bottom, use long tail to sew both to side of elephant head, approximately 4 rounds down from top. Sew a few stitches to connect the bigger and smaller ears so they are touching and become one larger ear. Do the same on both sides of head.

Tail:

Ch 11, sl st in second ch from hook and the remaining 9 chs, fasten off.

Knot 2 strands of Sky yarn through last ch so that when knotted it makes a short tassel of 4 strands.

Sew onto back bottom of body.

FREDDY THE *Fox*

Freddy just likes to have fun and hang with his other cute critter friends! Simple shapes with a few embellishments complete this character.

Size: 10 inches tall x 8 inches wide

Materials:

- Bernat Super Value Yarn in Pumpkin
- Bernat Super Value Yarn in Black
- Bernat Super Value Yarn in White
- Size H Crochet Hook
- 12mm Safety Eyes
- 18mm Safety Nose
- Poly-fil Fiber Stuffing
- Tapestry Needle

Body:

With Pumpkin yarn, create a magic ring, ch 1 and make 10 sc in ring, join to first sc, ch 1.

Round 2: 2 sc in each st around, join, ch 1. (20 sts)

Round 3: *2 sc in next st, sc in next st, repeat from * around, join, ch 1. (30 sts)

Round 4: Sc in each st around, join, ch 1.

Round 5: *2 sc in next st, sc in next 2 sts, repeat from * around, join, ch 1. (40 sts)

Round 6: Sc in each st around, join, ch 1.

Round 7: *2 sc in next st, sc in next 3 sts, repeat from * around, join, ch 1. (50 sts)

Rounds 8–19: Sc in each st around, join, ch 1.

Round 20: *Sc2tog, sc in next 3 sts, repeat from * around, join, ch 1. (40 sts)

Rounds 21–22: Sc in each st around, join, ch 1.

Round 23: *Sc2tog, sc in next 2 sts, repeat from * around, join, ch 1. (30 sts)

Rounds 24–25: Sc in each st around, join, ch 1.

Round 26: *Sc2tog, sc in next st, repeat from * around, join, ch 1. (20 sts)

Rounds 27–28: Sc in each st around, join, ch 1.

Round 29: Sc2tog around, join. (10 sts)

Fasten off leaving a long tail and stuff, leaving top open.

Head:

With Pumpkin yarn, create a magic ring, ch 1 and make 10 sc in ring, join to first sc, ch 1.

Round 2: 2 sc in each st around, join, ch 1. (20 sts)

Round 3: Sc in each st around, join, ch 1.

Round 4: *2 sc in next st, sc in next st, repeat from * around, join, ch 1. (30 sts)

Round 5: Sc in each st around, join, ch 1.

Round 6: *2 sc in next st, sc in next 2 sts, repeat from * around, join, ch 1. (40 sts)

Round 7: *2 sc in next st, sc in next 3 sts, repeat from * around, join, ch 1. (50 sts)

Rounds 8–15: Sc in each st around, join, ch 1.

Round 16: *Sc2tog, sc in next 3 sts, repeat from * around, join, ch 1. (40 sts)

Round 17: Sc in each st around, join, ch 1.

Round 18: *Sc2tog, sc in next 2 sts, repeat from * around, join, ch 1. (30 sts)

Round 19: Sc in each st around, join, ch 1.

Round 20: *Sc2tog, sc in next st, repeat from * around, join, ch 1. (20 sts)

Round 21: Sc in each st around, join, ch 1.

At this point attach the safety eyes. Then stuff before closing the head.

Round 22: Sc2tog around, join, ch 1. (10 sts)

Round 23: Sc2tog around, join. (5 sts)

Fasten off leaving a long tail.

Use long tail to close final round and weave in ends.

Use long tail of body to sew on head.

Legs (make 2):

With Black yarn, create a magic ring, ch 1 and make 6 sc in ring, join to first sc, ch 1.

Round 2: 2 sc in each st around, join, ch 2. (12 sts)

Round 3: 2 dc in first 3 sts, 2 hdc in next 2 sts, 2 sc in next 5 sts, 2 hdc in last 2 sts, join, ch 1. (24 sts)

Round 4: Working in back loops only for this round, sc in each st around, join, ch 1.

Rounds 5–6: Sc in each st around, join, ch 1.

Round 7: Sc2tog 6 times, sc in remaining 12 sts, join, ch 1. (18 sts)

Round 8: Sc in each st around, join, ch 1.

Round 9: Sc2tog 5 times, sc in remaining 8 sts, join, *change to Pumpkin yarn*, ch 1. (13 sts)

Rounds 10–14: Sc in each st around, join, ch 1.

Fasten off leaving a long tail and stuff.

Use long tail to sew onto bottom of body.

Arms (make 2):

With Black yarn, create a magic ring, ch 1 and make 10 sc in ring, join to first sc, ch 1.

Round 2: *2 sc in next st, sc in next st, repeat from * around, join, ch 1. (15 sts)

Rounds 3–4: Sc in each st around, join, ch 1.

Round 5: *Sc2tog, sc in next 3 sts, repeat from * around, join, ch 1. (12 sts)

Rounds 6-9: Sc in each st around, join, ch 1.

Change to Pumpkin yarn.

Rounds 10–22: Sc in each st around, join, ch 1.

Fasten off leaving a long tail and stuff.

Flatten opening and use long tail to sew onto body under the head.

Cheeks (make 2):

With White yarn, ch 10, sc in second ch from hook, sc in next ch, hdc in next ch, dc in next 2 chs, tc in next 2 chs, dc in next ch, hdc and sc in last ch.

Now working along other side of ch, sc in each ch across, do not join but continue to crochet another round. (18 sts)

Round 2: Sc in first 8 sts, 2 sc in next 3 sts, sc in remaining sts, join. (21 sts)

Fasten off leaving a long tail.

Use long tail to sew cheeks onto front of head. The two smaller points of the cheeks should touch each other.

Nose:

With White yarn, create a magic ring, ch 1 and make
6 sc in ring, join, ch 1.

Round 2: 2 sc in each st around, join, ch 1. (12 sts)

Rounds 3–5: Sc in each st around, join, ch 1.

Fasten off leaving a long tail.

Add safety nose to center of nose, stuff and use long
tail to sew onto head, overlapping the point where
the cheeks meet.

Ears (make 2):

With Black yarn, create a magic ring, ch 1 and make
4 sc in ring, join to first sc, ch 1.

Round 2: Sc in each st around, join, ch 1.

Round 3: 2 sc in each st around, join, *change to
Pumpkin yarn*, ch 1. (8 sts)

Round 4: Sc in each st around, join, ch 1.

Round 5: *2 sc in next st, sc in next st, repeat from *
around, join, ch 1. (12 sts)

Round 6: Sc in each st around, join, ch 1.

Round 7: *2 sc in next st, sc in next 2 sts, repeat
from * around, join, ch 1. (16 sts)

Rounds 8–9: Sc in each st around, join, ch 1.

Fasten off leaving a long tail.

No need to stuff. Use long tail to sew onto top sides
of head.

Tail:

With White yarn, create a magic ring, ch 1 and make
3 sc in ring, join to first sc, ch 1.

Round 2: 2 sc in each st around, join, ch 1. (6 sts)

Round 3: *2 sc in next st, sc in next st, repeat from *
around, join, ch 1. (9 sts)

Round 4: *2 sc in next st, sc in next 2 sts, repeat
from * around, join, ch 1. (12 sts)

Round 5: *2 sc in next st, sc in next 3 sts, repeat
from * around, join, ch 1. (15 sts)

Round 6: *2 sc in next st, sc in next 2 sts, repeat
from * around, join, ch 1. (20 sts)

Rounds 7–10: Sc in each st around, join, ch 1.
Change to Pumpkin yarn at end of round 10.

Rounds 11–13: Sc in each st around, join, ch 1.

Round 14: *Sc2tog, sc in next 2 sts, repeat from *
around, join, ch 1. (15 sts)

Round 15: Sc in each st around, join, ch 1.

Round 16: *Sc2tog, sc in next st, repeat from *
around, join, ch 1. (10 sts)

Rounds 16–21: Sc in each st around, join, ch 1.

Fasten off leaving a long tail and stuff.

Use long tail to sew onto bottom back of body.

GINGER THE *Giraffe*

She may be tall but she's such a gentle giant! Ginger the Giraffe has a lot of little parts and details but I have no doubt that she will be one of the most popular animals in your amigurumi zoo!

Size: 14 inches tall x 8 inches wide

Materials:
- Bernat Super Value Yarn in Bright Yellow
- Bernat Super Value Yarn in Taupe
- Bernat Super Value Yarn in Oatmeal
- Size H Crochet Hook
- 12mm Safety Eyes
- Poly-fil Fiber Stuffing
- Tapestry Needle
- Removable Stitch Marker (optional)

Body:

With Bright Yellow yarn, create a magic ring, ch 1 and make 10 sc in ring, join to first sc, ch 1.

Round 2: 2 sc in each st around, join, ch 1. (20 sts)

Round 3: *2 sc in next st, sc in next st, repeat from * around, join, ch 1. (30 sts)

Round 4: Sc in each st around, join, ch 1.

Round 5: *2 sc in next st, sc in next 2 sts, repeat from * around, join, ch 1. (40 sts)

Round 6: Sc in each st around, join, ch 1.

Round 7: *2 sc in next st, sc in next 3 sts, repeat from * around, join, ch 1. (50 sts)

Rounds 8–19: Sc in each st around, join, ch 1.

Round 20: *Sc2tog, sc in next 3 sts, repeat from * around, join, ch 1. (40 sts)

Rounds 21–22: Sc in each st around, join, ch 1.

Round 23: *Sc2tog, sc in next 2 sts, repeat from * around, join, ch 1. (30 sts)

Rounds 24–25: Sc in each st around, join, ch 1.

Round 26: *Sc2tog, sc in next st, repeat from * around, join, ch 1. (20 sts)

Rounds 27–34: Sc in each st around, join, ch 1.

Fasten off leaving a long tail and stuff, leaving top open.

Head:

With Bright Yellow yarn, create a magic ring, ch 1 and make 10 sc in ring, join to first sc, ch 1.

Round 2: 2 sc in each st around, join, ch 1. (20 sts)

Round 3: Sc in each st around, join, ch 1.

Round 4: *2 sc in next st, sc in next st, repeat from * around, join, ch 1. (30 sts)

Round 5: Sc in each st around, join, ch 1.

Round 6: *2 sc in next st, sc in next 2 sts, repeat from * around, join, ch 1. (40 sts)

Round 7: *2 sc in next st, sc in next 3 sts, repeat from * around, join, ch 1. (50 sts)

Rounds 8–15: Sc in each st around, join, ch 1.

Round 16: *Sc2tog, sc in next 3 sts, repeat from *
around, join, ch 1. (40 sts)

Round 17: Sc in each st around, join, ch 1.

Round 18: *Sc2tog, sc in next 2 sts, repeat from *
around, join, ch 1. (30 sts)

Round 19: Sc in each st around, join, ch 1.

Round 20: *Sc2tog, sc in next st, repeat from *
around, join, ch 1. (20 sts)

Round 21: Sc in each st around, join, ch 1.

*At this point attach the safety eyes between
rounds 9 and 10 (about 7 sts apart). Then stuff
before closing the head.*

Round 22: Sc2tog around, join, ch 1. (10 sts)

Round 23: Sc2tog around, join. (5 sts)

Fasten off leaving a long tail.

Use long tail to close final round and weave in ends.

Use long tail of body to sew on head.

Arms (make 2):

With Taupe yarn, create a magic ring, ch 1 and make
10 sc in ring, join to first sc, ch 1.

Round 2: *2 sc in next st, sc in next st, repeat from *
around, join, ch 1. (15 sts)

Rounds 3–4: Sc in each st around, join, ch 1.

Round 5: *Sc2tog, sc in next 3 sts, repeat from *
around, join, *change to Bright Yellow yarn*, ch 1.
(12 sts)

Rounds 6–22: Sc in each st around, join, ch 1.

Fasten off leaving a long tail and stuff.

Flatten opening and use long tail to sew onto body
at base of neck.

Legs (make 2):

With Taupe yarn, create a magic ring, ch 1 and make
6 sc in ring, join to first sc, ch 1.

Round 2: 2 sc in each st around, join, ch 2. (12 sts)

Round 3: 2 dc in first 3 sts, 2 hdc in next 2 sts, 2 sc in
next 5 sts, 2 hdc in last 2 sts, join, ch 1. (24 sts)

Round 4: Working in back loops only for this round,
sc in each st around, join, ch 1.

Round 5: Sc in each st around, join, *change to
Bright Yellow yarn*, ch 1.

Round 6: Sc in each st around, join, ch 1.

Round 7: Sc2tog 6 times, sc in remaining 12 sts, join,
ch 1. (18 sts)

Round 8: Sc in each st around, join, ch 1.

Round 9: Sc2tog 5 times, sc in remaining 8 sts, join,
ch 1. (13 sts)

Rounds 10–14: Sc in each st around, join, ch 1.

Fasten off leaving a long tail and stuff.

Use long tail to sew onto bottom of body.

Horns (make 2):

With Taupe yarn, create a magic ring, ch 1 and make
6 sc in ring, join to first sc, ch 1.

Stuff as you go.

Round 2: *2 sc in next st, sc in next st, repeat from *
around, join, ch 1. (9 sts)

Round 3: *2 sc in next st, sc in next 2 sts, repeat
from * around, join, ch 1. (12 sts)

Rounds 4–5: Sc in each st around, join, ch 1.

Round 6: *Sc2tog, sc in next 2 sts, repeat from
* around, join, *change to Bright Yellow yarn*,
ch 1. (9 sts)

Rounds 7–12: Sc in each st around, join, ch 1.
Fasten off leaving a long tail and sew onto top
  of head.

Ears (make 2):

With Bright Yellow yarn, ch 5, sc in second ch from
  hook and in remaining 3 chs, ch 1, turn. (4 sts)
Row 2: 2 sc in first st, sc in next 2 sts, 2 sc in last st,
  ch 1, turn. (6 sts)
Rows 3–5: Sc in each st across, ch 1, turn.
Row 6: Sc2tog, sc in next 2 sts, sc2tog, ch 1,
  turn. (4 sts)
Row 7: Sc in each st across, ch 1, turn.
Row 8: Sc2tog twice, then continue to sc around
  entire ear, join to the second sc, causing the
  ear to cup.
Fasten off leaving a long tail and sew onto head.

Snout:

With Oatmeal yarn, create a magic ring, ch 1 and
  make 10 sc in ring, join to first sc, ch 1.
Round 2: 2 sc in each st around, join, ch 1. (20 sts)
Round 3: Sc in each st around, join, ch 1.
Round 4: *2 sc in next st, sc in next st, repeat from *
  around, join, ch 1. (30 sts)
Rounds 5–7: Sc in each st around, join, ch 1.
Fasten off after leaving a long tail and stuff.
Use long tail to sew onto front of head directly
  under eyes.

Spots (make 6 or more):

With Taupe yarn, create a magic ring, make 6 sc in
  ring, continue to work in spiral form without joining or ch 1 until indicated. Use a removable stitch
  marker to indicate beginning of round if needed.
Round 2: *2 sc in next st, sc in next st, repeat from *
  around. (9 sts)
Round 3: 2 hdc in next st, 2 dc in next st, 2 hdc in
  next st, sc + hdc + hdc in next st, sc in next st, sl st
  to join to next st, ending round early.
Fasten off leaving a long tail and sew sporadically
  onto giraffe head and body.

Tail:

With Bright Yellow yarn, ch 11, sl st in second ch
  from hook and remaining 9 chs, fasten off.
Knot 4 strands of Taupe yarn through last ch so
  that when knotted it makes a short tassel of
  8 strands.
Sew onto back bottom of body.

HENRIETTA THE *Hippo*

Hip Hip Hippo-Hooray! Henrietta is pretty in purple and worked up in all one color. You only need one skein of yarn to make this plush hippo.

Size: 10 inches tall x 8 inches wide

Materials:

- Bernat Super Value Yarn in Lilac
- Size H Crochet Hook
- 12mm Safety Eyes
- Poly-fil Fiber Stuffing
- Tapestry Needle

Body:

Create a magic ring, ch 1 and make 10 sc in ring, join to first sc, ch 1.

Round 2: 2 sc in each st around, join, ch 1. (20 sts)

Round 3: *2 sc in next st, sc in next st, repeat from * around, join, ch 1. (30 sts)

Round 4: Sc in each st around, join, ch 1.

Round 5: *2 sc in next st, sc in next 2 sts, repeat from * around, join, ch 1. (40 sts)

Round 6: Sc in each st around, join, ch 1.

Round 7: *2 sc in next st, sc in next 3 sts, repeat from * around, join, ch 1. (50 sts)

Rounds 8–19: Sc in each st around, join, ch 1.

Round 20: *Sc2tog, sc in next 3 sts, repeat from * around, join, ch 1. (40 sts)

Rounds 21–22: Sc in each st around, join, ch 1.

Round 23: *Sc2tog, sc in next 2 sts, repeat from * around, join, ch 1. (30 sts)

Rounds 24–25: Sc in each st around, join, ch 1.

Round 26: *Sc2tog, sc in next st, repeat from * around, join, ch 1. (20 sts)

Rounds 27–28: Sc in each st around, join, ch 1.

Round 29: Sc2tog around, join. (10 sts)

Fasten off leaving a long tail and stuff, leaving top open.

Head:

Create a magic ring, ch 1 and make 10 sc in ring, join to first sc, ch 1.

Round 2: 2 sc in each st around, join, ch 1. (20 sts)

Round 3: Sc in each st around, join, ch 1.

Round 4: *2 sc in next st, sc in next st, repeat from * around, join, ch 1. (30 sts)

Round 5: Sc in each st around, join, ch 1.

Round 6: *2 sc in next st, sc in next 2 sts, repeat from * around, join, ch 1. (40 sts)

Round 7: *2 sc in next st, sc in next 3 sts, repeat from * around, join, ch 1. (50 sts)

Rounds 8–15: Sc in each st around, join, ch 1.

Round 16: *Sc2tog, sc in next 3 sts, repeat from * around, join, ch 1. (40 sts)

Round 17: Sc in each st around, join, ch 1.

Round 18: *Sc2tog, sc in next 2 sts, repeat from *
around, join, ch 1. (30 sts)

Round 19: Sc in each st around, join, ch 1.

Round 20: *Sc2tog, sc in next st, repeat from *
around, join, ch 1. (20 sts)

Round 21: Sc in each st around, join, ch 1.

*At this point attach the safety eyes. Then stuff
before closing the head.*

Round 22: Sc2tog around, join, ch 1. (10 sts)

Round 23: Sc2tog around, join. (5 sts)

Fasten off leaving a long tail.

Use long tail to close final round and weave in ends.

Use long tail of body to sew on head.

Legs (make 2):

Create a magic ring, ch 1 and make 6 sc in ring, join
to first sc, ch 1.

Round 2: 2 sc in each st around, join, ch 2. (12 sts)

Round 3: 2 dc in first 3 sts, 2 hdc in next 2 sts, 2 sc in
next 5 sts, 2 hdc in last 2 sts, join, ch 1. (24 sts)

Round 4: Working in back loops only for this round,
sc in each st around, join, ch 1.

Rounds 5–6: Sc in each st around, join, ch 1.

Round 7: Sc2tog 6 times, sc in remaining 12 sts, join,
ch 1. (18 sts)

Round 8: Sc in each st around, join, ch 1.

Round 9: Sc2tog 5 times, sc in remaining 8 sts, join,
ch 1. (13 sts)

Rounds 10–14: Sc in each st around, join, ch 1.

Fasten off leaving a long tail and stuff.

Use long tail to sew onto bottom of body.

Arms (make 2):

Create a magic ring, ch 1 and make 10 sc in ring, join
to first sc, ch 1.

Round 2: *2 sc in next st, sc in next st, repeat from *
around, join, ch 1. (15 sts)

Rounds 3–4: Sc in each st around, join, ch 1.

Round 5: *Sc2tog, sc in next 3 sts, repeat from *
around, join, ch 1. (12 sts)

Rounds 6–22: Sc in each st around, join, ch 1.

Fasten off leaving a long tail and stuff.

Flatten opening and use long tail to sew onto body
under the head.

Snout:

Ch 11, sc in second ch from hook and next 8 chs,
3 sc in last ch.

Now working on other side of ch, sc in first 9 chs,
3 sc in last ch, join, ch 1. (24 sts)

Round 2: Sc in first 9 sts, 2 sc in next 3 sts, sc in next
9 sts, 2 sc in last 3 sts, join, ch 1. (30 sts)

Rounds 3–8: Sc in each st around, join, ch 1.

Fasten off leaving a long tail and stuff.

Use long tail to sew onto head directly below
the eyes.

Nostrils (make 2):

Create a magic ring, ch 1 and make 6 sc in ring, join
to first sc, fasten off leaving a long tail.

Use long tail to sew nostrils onto snout.

Ears (make 2):

Create a magic ring, ch 1 and make 10 sc in ring, join to first sc, ch 1.

Round 2: *2 sc in first st, sc in next st, repeat from * around, join, ch 1. (15 sts)

Rounds 3–4: Sc in each st around, join, ch 1.

Round 5: *Sc2tog, sc in next st, repeat from * around, join, ch 1. (10 sts)

Round 6: Sc in each st around, join.

Fasten off leaving a long tail.

No need to stuff ears. Pinch bottom of ears and use long tail to sew closed, then sew onto head (about 5 rows down from top on either side).

IGGY THE *Iguana*

Iggy is itching to get on your crochet hook! He's chubby and cuddly and just about the cutest reptile you will ever lay eyes on!

Size: 5 inches tall x 19 inches long

Materials:
- Bernat Super Value Yarn in Soft Fern (light green)
- Bernat Super Value Yarn in Lush (dark green)
- Size H Crochet Hook
- 12mm Safety Eyes
- Poly-fil Fiber Stuffing
- Tapestry Needle

Body and Tail:

With Soft Fern yarn, create a magic ring, ch 1 and make 10 sc in ring, join to first sc, ch 1.

Round 2: 2 sc in each st around, join, ch 1. (20 sts)

Round 3: Sc in each st around, join, ch 1.

Round 4: *2 sc in next st, sc in next st, repeat from * around, join, ch 1. (30 sts)

Round 5: Sc in each st around, join, ch 1.

Round 6: *2 sc in next st, sc in next 2 sts, repeat from * around, join, ch 1. (40 sts)

Round 7: *2 sc in next st, sc in next 3 sts, repeat from * around, join, ch 1. (50 sts)

Rounds 8–15: Sc in each st around, join, ch 1.

Round 16: *Sc2tog, sc in next 3 sts, repeat from * around, join, ch 1. (40 sts)

Round 17: Sc in each st around, join, ch 1.

Round 18: *Sc2tog, sc in next 2 sts, repeat from * around, join, ch 1. (30 sts)

Round 19: Sc in each st around, join, ch 1.

Round 20: *Sc2tog, sc in next st, repeat from * around, join, ch 1. (20 sts)

Rounds 21–23: Sc in each st around, join, ch 1.
Change to Lush yarn, then continue to alternate between colors every 3 rounds.

Rounds 24–39: Sc in each st around, join, ch 1.

Round 40: *Sc2tog, sc in next 2 sts, repeat from * around, join, ch 1. (15 sts)

Rounds 41–42: Sc in each st around, join, ch 1.

Round 43: *Sc2tog, sc in next st, repeat from * around, join, ch 1. (10 sts)

Round 44: Sc in each st around, join, *change to Soft Fern yarn and continue with it until end*, ch 1.

Rounds 45–47: Sc in each st around, join, ch 1.

Round 48: Sc2tog around, join. (5 sts)

Fasten off leaving a long tail.

Use long tail to close final round and weave in ends.

Head:

With Soft Fern yarn, create a magic ring, ch 1 and make 10 sc in ring, join to first sc, ch 1.

Round 2: 2 sc in each st around, join, ch 1. (20 sts)

Round 3: Sc in each st around, join, ch 1.

Round 4: *2 sc in next st, sc in next st, repeat from * around, join, ch 1. (30 sts)

Round 5: Sc in each st around, join, ch 1.

Round 6: *2 sc in next st, sc in next 2 sts, repeat from * around, join, ch 1. (40 sts)

Round 7: *2 sc in next st, sc in next 3 sts, repeat from * around, join, ch 1. (50 sts)

Rounds 8–15: Sc in each st around, join, ch 1.

Round 16: *Sc2tog, sc in next 3 sts, repeat from * around, join, ch 1. (40 sts)

Round 17: Sc in each st around, join, ch 1.

Round 18: *Sc2tog, sc in next 2 sts, repeat from * around, join, ch 1. (30 sts)

Round 19: Sc in each st around, join, ch 1.

Round 20: *Sc2tog, sc in next st, repeat from * around, join, ch 1. (20 sts)

Rounds 21–24: Sc in each st around, join, ch 1.

At this point attach the safety eyes between rounds 14 and 15 (about 10 sts apart). Then stuff before closing the head.

Round 25: Sc2tog around, join, ch 1. (10 sts)

Round 26: Sc2tog around, join. (5 sts)

Fasten off leaving a long tail.

Use long tail to close final round and weave in ends.

Use long tail of body to sew on head.

Spikes:

With Lush yarn, ch 37, sc in second ch from hook, hdc in next ch, dc in next ch, skip 2 chs and join to next ch with a sl st, *ch 4, sc in second ch from hook, hdc in next ch, dc in last ch, skip 2 chs, join with a sl st, repeat from * across remaining chs, making a total of 11 spikes.

Fasten off leaving a long tail and sew onto back and part of head.

Legs (make 4):

With Soft Fern yarn, create a magic ring, ch 1 and make 6 sc in ring, join to first sc, ch 1.

Round 2: 2 sc in each st around, join, ch 2. (12 sts)

Round 3: 2 dc in first 3 sts, 2 hdc in next 2 sts, 2 sc in next 5 sts, 2 hdc in last 2 sts, join, ch 1. (24 sts)

Round 4: Working in back loops only for this round, sc in each st around, join, ch 1.

Rounds 5–6: Sc in each st around, join, ch 1.

Round 7: Sc2tog 6 times, sc in remaining 12 sts, join, ch 1. (18 sts)

Round 8: Sc in each st around, join, ch 1.

Round 9: Sc2tog 5 times, sc in remaining 8 sts, join, ch 1. (13 sts)

Rounds 10–11: Sc in each st around, join, ch 1.

Fasten off leaving a long tail and stuff.

Use long tail to sew onto bottom of body.

JUNIOR THE *Jellyfish*

Junior the Jellyfish is the baby of the group. He is small, sweet, and always smiling! His curly coils will wrap around you for lots of cuddle time.

Size: 19 inches tall (including coils) or 7 inches tall without coils x 5 inches wide

Materials:

- Bernat Super Value Yarn in Aqua
- Bernat Super Value Yarn in Black
- Size H Crochet Hook
- 12mm Safety Eyes
- Poly-fil Fiber Stuffing
- Tapestry Needle

Body:

Create a magic ring, ch 1 and make 10 sc in ring, join to first sc, ch 1.

Round 2: 2 sc in each st around, join, ch 1. (20 sts)

Round 3: *2 sc in next st, sc in next st, repeat from * around, join, ch 1. (30 sts)

Round 4: Sc in each st around, join, ch 1.

Round 5: *2 sc in next st, sc in next 2 sts, repeat from * around, join, ch 1. (40 sts)

Round 6: Sc in each st around, join, ch 1.

Round 7: *2 sc in next st, sc in next 3 sts, repeat from * around, join, ch 1. (50 sts)

Rounds 8–19: Sc in each st around, join, ch 1.

Round 20: Sc2tog, sc in next 3 sts, repeat from * around, join, ch 1. (40 sts)

Rounds 21–22: Sc in each st around, join, ch 1.

Round 23: Sc2tog, sc in next 2 sts, repeat from * around, join, ch 1. (30 sts)

Rounds 24–25: Sc in each st around, join, ch 1.

Round 26: Sc2tog, sc in next st, repeat from * around, join, ch 1. (20 sts)

Rounds 27–28: Sc in each st around, join, ch 1.

At this point attach the safety eyes (about 13 rounds up from bottom) and use Black yarn to sew on a smile (about 8 rounds up from bottom). Then make the scallops.

Round 29: *4 dc in next st, sl st in next st, repeat from * around, join. (40 sts)

Fasten off leaving a long tail. Stuff firmly, leaving bottom open.

Bottom of Body:

Create a magic ring, ch 1 and make 10 sc in ring, join to first sc, ch 1.

Round 2: 2 sc in each st around, join, ch 1. (20 sts)

Rounds 3–4: Sc in each st around, join, ch 1.

Fasten off leaving a long tail.

Coils (make 7):

Ch 60, 2 sc in second ch from hook and all remaining chs, then fasten off leaving a long tail.

Use long tail to sew coils to bottom of jellyfish body piece.

Use long tail to sew of bottom of jellyfish body to opening left on bottom of main body, closing the body.

KATIE THE *Kangaroo*

You will find Katie the Kangaroo jumping and hopping around all day! She works up in almost one solid color with just a contrasting color pocket. Use the pocket to store little keepsakes!

Size: 10 inches tall x 8 inches wide

Materials:

- Bernat Super Value Yarn in Topaz
- Bernat Super Value Yarn in Oatmeal
- Size H Crochet Hook
- 12mm Safety Eyes
- 18mm Safety Nose
- Poly-fil Fiber Stuffing
- Tapestry Needle

Body:

With Topaz yarn, create a magic ring, ch 1 and make 10 sc in ring, join to first sc, ch 1.

Round 2: 2 sc in each st around, join, ch 1. (20 sts)

Round 3: *2 sc in next st, sc in next st, repeat from * around, join, ch 1. (30 sts)

Round 4: Sc in each st around, join, ch 1.

Round 5: *2 sc in next st, sc in next 2 sts, repeat from * around, join, ch 1. (40 sts)

Round 6: Sc in each st around, join, ch 1.

Round 7: *2 sc in next st, sc in next 3 sts, repeat from * around, join, ch 1. (50 sts)

Rounds 8–19: Sc in each st around, join, ch 1.

Round 20: *Sc2tog, sc in next 3 sts, repeat from * around, join, ch 1. (40 sts)

Rounds 21–22: Sc in each st around, join, ch 1.

Round 23: *Sc2tog, sc in next 2 sts, repeat from * around, join, ch 1. (30 sts)

Rounds 24–25: Sc in each st around, join, ch 1.

Round 26: *Sc2tog, sc in next st, repeat from * around, join, ch 1. (20 sts)

Rounds 27–28: Sc in each st around, join, ch 1.

Round 29: Sc2tog around, join. (10 sts)

Fasten off leaving a long tail and stuff, leaving top open.

Head:

With Topaz yarn, create a magic ring, ch 1 and make 10 sc in ring, join to first sc, ch 1.

Round 2: 2 sc in each st around, join, ch 1. (20 sts)

Round 3: Sc in each st around, join, ch 1.

Round 4: *2 sc in next st, sc in next st, repeat from * around, join, ch 1. (30 sts)

Round 5: Sc in each st around, join, ch 1.

Round 6: *2 sc in next st, sc in next 2 sts, repeat from * around, join, ch 1. (40 sts)

Round 7: *2 sc in next st, sc in next 3 sts, repeat from * around, join, ch 1. (50 sts)

Rounds 8–15: Sc in each st around, join, ch 1.

Round 16: *Sc2tog, sc in next 3 sts, repeat from * around, join, ch 1. (40 sts)

Round 17: Sc in each st around, join, ch 1.

Round 18: *Sc2tog, sc in next 2 sts, repeat from * around, join, ch 1. (30 sts)

Round 19: Sc in each st around, join, ch 1.

Round 20: *Sc2tog, sc in next st, repeat from * around, join, ch 1. (20 sts)

Rounds 21–24: Sc in each st around, join, ch 1.

At this point attach the safety eyes between rounds 19 and 20 (about 7 sts apart). Add the safety nose between rounds 24 and 25 Then stuff before closing the head.

Round 25: Sc2tog around, join, ch 1. (10 sts)

Round 26: Sc2tog around, join. (5 sts)

Fasten off leaving a long tail.

Use long tail to close final round and weave in ends.

Use long tail of body to sew on head.

Legs (make 2):

With Topaz yarn, create a magic ring, ch 1 and make 6 sc in ring, join to first sc, ch 1.

Round 2: 2 sc in each st around, join, ch 2. (12 sts)

Round 3: 2 dc in first 3 sts, 2 hdc in next 2 sts, 2 sc in next 5 sts, 2 hdc in last 2 sts, join, ch 1. (24 sts)

Round 4: Working in back loops only for this round, sc in each st around, join, ch 1.

Rounds 5–6: Sc in each st around, join, ch 1.

Round 7: Sc2tog 6 times, sc in remaining 12 sts, join, ch 1. (18 sts)

Round 8: Sc in each st around, join, ch 1.

Round 9: Sc2tog 5 times, sc in remaining 8 sts, join, ch 1. (13 sts)

Rounds 10–14: Sc in each st around, join, ch 1.

Fasten off leaving a long tail and stuff.

Use long tail to sew onto bottom of body.

Arms (make 2):

With Topaz yarn, create a magic ring, ch 1 and make 10 sc in ring, join to first sc, ch 1.

Round 2: *2 sc in next st, sc in next st, repeat from * around, join, ch 1. (15 sts)

Rounds 3–4: Sc in each st around, join, ch 1.

Round 5: *Sc2tog, sc in next 3 sts, repeat from * around, join, ch 1. (12 sts)

Rounds 6–22: Sc in each st around, join, ch 1.

Fasten off leaving a long tail and stuff.

Flatten opening and use long tail to sew onto body under the head.

Ears (make 2):

With Topaz yarn, create a magic ring, make 4 sc in ring, join to first sc, ch 1.

Round 2: 2 sc in each st around, join, ch 1. (8 sts)

Round 3: Sc in each st around, join, ch 1.

Round 4: *2 sc in next st, sc in next st, repeat from * around, join, ch 1. (12 sts)

Round 5: Sc in each st around, join, ch 1.

Round 6: *2 sc in next st, sc in next 2 sts, join, ch 1. (16 sts)

Rounds 7–8: Sc in each st around, join, ch 1.

Round 9: *Sc2tog, sc in next 2 sts, join, ch 1. (12 sts)

Round 10: Sc in each st around, join.

Fasten off leaving a long tail.

No need to stuff. Use long tail to sew onto top sides of head.

Tail:

With Topaz yarn, create a magic ring, make 6 sc in
  ring, join to first sc, ch 1.

Round 2: Sc in each st around, join, ch 1.

Round 3: *2 sc in next st, sc in next st, repeat from *
  around, join, ch 1. (9 sts)

Round 4: Sc in each st around, join, ch 1.

Round 5: *2 sc in next st, sc in next 2 sts, join,
  ch 1. (12 sts)

Rounds 6–7: Sc in each st around, join, ch 1.

Round 8: *2 sc in next st, sc in next 3 sts, repeat
  from * around, join, ch 1. (15 sts)

Rounds 9–10: Sc in each st around, join, ch 1.

Round 11: *2 sc in next st, sc in next 4 sts, repeat
  from * around, join, ch 1. (18 sts)

Rounds 12–18: Sc in each st around, join, ch 1.

Fasten off leaving a long tail and stuff.

Use long tail to sew onto back of body.

Pocket:

With Oatmeal yarn, ch 11, sc in second ch from
  hook and the remaining 9 chs, ch 1, turn. (10 sts)

Row 2: 2 sc in first st, sc in next 8 sts, 2 sc in last st,
  ch 1, turn. (12 sts)

Rows 3–10: Sc in each st across, ch 1, turn.

After last row, do not ch 1 and continue to sc
  around 3 edges of the pocket, leaving top open.

Fasten off leaving a long tail and sew the pocket
  onto the belly, leaving the top open.

LILLY THE *Lamb*

Ba-ba-ba-beautiful little Lilly the Lamb is ready to leap onto your hook! The perfect gift and an adorable addition to the cute critters set!

Size: 10 inches tall x 8 inches wide

Materials:
- Bernat Super Value Yarn in White
- Bernat Super Value Yarn in Soft Gray
- Bernat Super Value Yarn in Black
- Size H Crochet Hook
- 12mm Safety Eyes
- Poly-fil Fiber Stuffing
- Tapestry Needle

Body:

With White yarn, create a magic ring, ch 1 and make 10 sc in ring, join to first sc, ch 1.

Round 2: 2 sc in each st around, join, ch 1. (20 sts)

Round 3: *2 sc in next st, sc in next st, repeat from * around, join, ch 1. (30 sts)

Round 4: Sc in each st around, join, ch 1.

Round 5: *2 sc in next st, sc in next 2 sts, repeat from * around, join, ch 1. (40 sts)

Round 6: Sc in each st around, join, ch 1.

Round 7: *2 sc in next st, sc in next 3 sts, repeat from * around, join, ch 1. (50 sts)

Rounds 8–19: Sc in each st around, join, ch 1.

Round 20: *Sc2tog, sc in next 3 sts, repeat from * around, join, ch 1. (40 sts)

Rounds 21–22: Sc in each st around, join, ch 1.

Round 23: *Sc2tog, sc in next 2 sts, repeat from * around, join, ch 1. (30 sts)

Rounds 24–25: Sc in each st around, join, ch 1.

Round 26: *Sc2tog, sc in next st, repeat from * around, join, ch 1. (20 sts)

Rounds 27–28: Sc in each st around, join, ch 1.

Round 29: Sc2tog around, join. (10 sts)

Fasten off leaving a long tail and stuff, leaving top open.

Head:

With White yarn, create a magic ring, ch 1 and make 10 sc in ring, join to first sc, ch 1.

Round 2: 2 sc in each st around, join, ch 1. (20 sts)

Round 3: Sc in each st around, join, ch 1.

Round 4: *2 sc in next st, sc in next st, repeat from * around, join, ch 1. (30 sts)

Round 5: Sc in each st around, join, ch 1.

Round 6: *2 sc in next st, sc in next 2 sts, repeat from * around, join, ch 1. (40 sts)

Round 7: *2 sc in next st, sc in next 3 sts, repeat from * around, join, ch 1. (50 sts)

Rounds 8–15: Sc in each st around, join, ch 1.

Round 16: *Sc2tog, sc in next 3 sts, repeat from * around, join, *change to Soft Gray yarn*, ch 1. (40 sts)

Round 17: Sc in each st around, join, ch 1.

Round 18: *Sc2tog, sc in next 2 sts, repeat from * around, join, ch 1. (30 sts)

Round 19: Sc in each st around, join, ch 1.

Round 20: *Sc2tog, sc in next st, repeat from * around, join, ch 1. (20 sts)

Rounds 21–24: Sc in each st around, join, ch 1.

At this point attach the safety eyes between rounds 19 and 20 (about 7 sts apart). Then stuff before closing the head.

Round 25: Sc2tog around, join, ch 1. (10 sts)

Round 26: Sc2tog around, join. (5 sts)

Fasten off leaving a long tail.

Use long tail to close final round and weave in ends.

Use long tail of body to sew on head. Head will sit "sideways" on body, with the white in the back and gray nose pointing to the front.

Use Black yarn to stitch on a little nose.

Legs (make 2):

With Soft Gray yarn, create a magic ring, ch 1 and make 6 sc in ring, join to first sc, ch 1.

Round 2: 2 sc in each st around, join, ch 2. (12 sts)

Round 3: 2 dc in first 3 sts, 2 hdc in next 2 sts, 2 sc in next 5 sts, 2 hdc in last 2 sts, join, ch 1. (24 sts)

Round 4: Working in back loops only for this round, sc in each st around, join, ch 1.

Rounds 5–6: Sc in each st around, join, ch 1.

Round 7: Sc2tog 6 times, sc in remaining 12 sts, join, ch 1. (18 sts)

Round 8: Sc in each st around, join, ch 1.

Round 9: Sc2tog 5 times, sc in remaining 8 sts, join, ch 1. (13 sts)

Rounds 10–14: Sc in each st around, join, ch 1.

Fasten off leaving a long tail and stuff.

Use long tail to sew onto bottom of body.

Arms (make 2):

With Soft Gray yarn, create a magic ring, ch 1 and make 10 sc in ring, join to first sc, ch 1.

Round 2: *2 sc in next st, sc in next st, repeat from * around, join, ch 1. (15 sts)

Rounds 3–4: Sc in each st around, join, ch 1.

Round 5: *Sc2tog, sc in next 3 sts, repeat from * around, join, ch 1. (12 sts)

Rounds 6–22: Sc in each st around, join, ch 1.

Fasten off leaving a long tail and stuff.

Flatten opening and use long tail to sew onto body under the head.

Ears (make 2):

Outer Ear (make 2):

With White yarn, ch 8, hdc in second ch from hook and in the next 5 chs, make 2 hdc in last ch.

Now working on other side of ch, hdc in each ch, join to first hdc, ch 2. (14 sts)

Round 2: 2 dc in the first 3 sts, 2 hdc in next st, 2 sc in the next 8 sts, 2 hdc in next st, 2 dc in last st, join. (28 sts)

Fasten off leaving a long tail to sew ear onto head.

Inner Ear (make 2):

With Soft Gray yarn, ch 6, sc in second ch from hook and in the next 3 sts, 2 sc in last ch.

Now working on other side of the ch, sc in each ch, join to first sc, ch 2. (11 sts)

Round 2: 2 dc in the first 2 sts, 2 hdc in next st, 2 sc in next 6 sts, 2 hdc in next st, 2 dc in last st, join. (22 sts)

Fasten off leaving a long tail and sew inner ear inside the outer ear.

After sewing the inner ear into the outer ear, pinch the smaller end together and use long tail of outer ear to sew some of it shut before you sew it onto the sides of the head.

MAX THE *Monkey*

Time to monkey around with this silly amigurumi named Max! Stitch him up with a smile and a long swinging tail. It's all monkey business when you are crocheting this cute plushie.

Size: 10 inches tall x 8 inches wide

Materials:
- Bernat Super Value Yarn in Taupe (dark brown)
- Bernat Super Value Yarn in Oatmeal (light brown)
- Size H Crochet Hook
- 12mm Safety Eyes
- 18mm Safety Nose
- Poly-fil Fiber Stuffing
- Tapestry Needle

Body:

With Taupe yarn, create a magic ring, ch 1 and make 10 sc in ring, join to first sc, ch 1.

Round 2: 2 sc in each st around, join, ch 1. (20 sts)

Round 3: *2 sc in next st, sc in next st, repeat from * around, join, ch 1. (30 sts)

Round 4: Sc in each st around, join, ch 1.

Round 5: *2 sc in next st, sc in next 2 sts, repeat from * around, join, ch 1. (40 sts)

Round 6: Sc in each st around, join, ch 1.

Round 7: *2 sc in first st, sc in next 3 sts, repeat from * around, join, ch 1. (50 sts)

Rounds 8–19: Sc in each st around, join, ch 1.

Round 20: *Sc2tog, sc in next 3 sts, repeat from * around, join, ch 1. (40 sts)

Rounds 21–22: Sc in each st around, join, ch 1.

Round 23: *Sc2tog, sc in next 2 sts, repeat from * around, join, ch 1. (30 sts)

Rounds 24–25: Sc in each st around, join, ch 1.

Round 26: Sc2tog, sc in next st, repeat from * around, join, ch 1. (20 sts)

Rounds 27–28: Sc in each st around, join, ch 1.

Round 29: Sc2tog around, join. (10 sts)

Fasten off leaving a long tail and stuff, leaving top open.

Eye Piece:

With Oatmeal yarn, ch 11, sc in second ch from hook, hdc + dc in next ch, 2 dc in next ch, dc + hdc in next ch, sl st in next ch, sc in next ch, hdc + dc in next ch, 2 dc in next ch, dc + hdc in next ch, sc in last ch.

Now working on the other side of ch, sc in each ch, fasten off leaving a long tail.

Snout:

With Oatmeal yarn, ch 11, sc in second ch from hook and next 8 chs, 3 sc in last ch.

Now working on other side of ch, sc in first 9 chs, 3 sc in last ch, join to first sc, ch 1. (24 sts)

Round 2: Sc in first 9 sts, 2 sc in next 3 sts, sc in next 9 sts, 2 sc in last 3 sts, join, ch 1. (30 sts)

Rounds 3–6: Sc in each st around, join, ch 1.

Fasten off leaving a long tail.

Stitch on a smile using Taupe yarn and place the safety nose, used upside down.

Head:

With Taupe yarn, create a magic ring, ch 1 and make 10 sc in ring, join to first sc, ch 1.

Round 2: *2 sc in each st around, join, ch 1. (20 sts)

Round 3: Sc in each st around, join, ch 1.

Round 4: *2 sc in next st, sc in next st, repeat from * around, join, ch 1. (30 sts)

Round 5: Sc in each st around, join, ch 1.

Round 6: *2 sc in next st, sc in next 2 sts, repeat from * around, join, ch 1. (40 sts)

Round 7: *2 sc in next st, sc in next 3 sts, repeat from * around, join, ch 1. (50 sts)

Rounds 8–15: Sc in each st around, join, ch 1.

Round 16: *Sc2tog, sc in next 3 sts, repeat from * around, join, ch 1. (40 sts)

Round 17: Sc in each st around, join, ch 1.

Round 18: *Sc2tog, sc in next 2 sts, repeat from * around, join, ch 1. (30 sts)

Round 19: Sc in each st around, join, ch 1.

Round 20: *Sc2tog, sc in next st, repeat from * around, join, ch 1. (20 sts)

Round 21: Sc in each st around, join, ch 1.

At this point attach the snout, eye piece, and safety eyes. Add safety eyes to eye piece. Use long tail to sew onto head. Stuff snout and use long tail to sew onto head directly below eye piece, overlapping slightly. Then stuff before closing the head.

Round 22: Sc2tog around, join, ch 1.

Round 23: Sc2tog around, join. (5 sts)

Fasten off leaving a long tail.

Use long tail to close final round and weave in ends.

Use long tail of body to sew on head.

Legs (make 2):

With Oatmeal yarn, create a magic ring, ch 1 and make 6 sc in ring, join to first sc, ch 1.

Round 2: 2 sc in each st around, join, ch 2. (12 sts)

Round 3: 2 dc in first 3 sts, 2 hdc in next 2 sts, 2 sc in next 5 sts, 2 hdc in last 2 sts, join, ch 1. (24 sts)

Round 4: Working in back loops only for this round, sc in each st around, join, *change to Taupe yarn*, ch 1.

Rounds 5–6: Sc in each st around, join, ch 1.

Round 7: Sc2tog 6 times, sc in remaining 12 sts, join, ch 1. (18 sts)

Round 8: Sc in each st around, join, ch 1.

Round 9: Sc2tog 5 times, sc in remaining 8 sts, join, ch 1. (13 sts)

Rounds 10–14: Sc in each st around, join, ch 1.

Fasten off leaving a long tail and stuff.

Use long tail to sew onto bottom of body.

Arms (make 2):

With Oatmeal yarn, create a magic ring, ch 1 and make 10 sc in ring, join to first sc, ch 1.

Round 2: *2 sc in next st, sc in next st, repeat from * around, join, ch 1. (15 sts)

Rounds 3–4: Sc in each st around, join, ch 1.

Round 5: *Sc2tog, sc in next 3 sts, repeat from * around, join, *change to Taupe yarn*, ch 1. (12 sts)

Rounds 6–22: Sc in each st around, join, ch 1.

Fasten off leaving a long tail and stuff.

Flatten opening and use long tail to sew onto body under the head.

Ears (make 2):

Outer Ear (make 2):

With Taupe yarn, create a magic ring, ch 1 and make 8 sc in ring, join to first sc, ch 1.

Round 2: 2 sc in each st around, join, ch 1. (16 sts)

Round 3: *2 sc in next st, sc in next 3 sts, repeat from * around, join, ch 1. (20 sts)

Rounds 4–7: Sc in each st around, join, ch 1.

Round 8: *Sc2tog, sc in next 3 sts, repeat from * around, join, ch 1. (16 sts)

Round 9: *Sc2tog, sc in next 2 sts, repeat from * around, join. (12 sts)

Fasten off leaving a long tail.

Do not stuff.

Inner Ear (make 2):

With Oatmeal yarn, create a magic ring, ch 1 and make 6 sc in ring, join to first sc, ch 1.

Round 2: *2 sc in next st, sc in next st, repeat from * around, join, ch 1. (9 sts)

Round 3: 2 sc in each st around, join. (18 sts)

Fasten off leaving a long tail and sew inner ear inside outer ear.

Use long tail from outer ear to sew ears onto sides of head.

Tail:

With Taupe yarn, create a magic ring, ch 1 and make 6 sc in ring, join to first sc, ch 1.

Rounds 2–28: Sc in each st around, join, ch 1.

Fasten off leaving a long tail.

No need to stuff.

Use long tail to sew onto back bottom of body.

NINA THE *Nightingale*

This sweet songbird will sing beautiful melodies from her yellow beak! Okay maybe you won't hear real music from this plushie but it's easy to imagine Nina the Nightingale's soothing sounds. Crochet her up in no time at all using a mix of patterns from her other animal friends!

Size: 12 inches tall x 6 inches wide

Materials:
- Bernat Super Value Yarn in Sky
- Bernat Super Value Yarn in Bright Yellow
- Size H Crochet Hook
- 12mm Safety Eyes
- Poly-fil Fiber Stuffing
- Tapestry Needle

Head:

With Sky yarn, create a magic ring, ch 1 and make 10 sc in ring, join to first sc, ch 1.

Round 2: 2 sc in each st around, join, ch 1. (20 sts)

Round 3: Sc in each st around, join, ch 1.

Round 4: *2 sc in next st, sc in next st, repeat from * around, join, ch 1. (30 sts)

Round 5: Sc in each st around, join, ch 1.

Round 6: *2 sc in next st, sc in next 2 sts, repeat from * around, join, ch 1. (40 sts)

Round 7: *2 sc in next st, sc in next 3 sts, repeat from * around, join, ch 1. (50 sts)

Rounds 8–15: Sc in each st around, join, ch 1.

Round 16: *Sc2tog, sc in next 3 sts, repeat from * around, join, ch 1. (40 sts)

Round 17: Sc in each st around, join, ch 1.

Round 18: *Sc2tog, sc in next 2 sts, repeat from * around, join, ch 1. (30 sts)

Round 19: Sc in each st around, join, ch 1.

Round 20: *Sc2tog, sc in next st, repeat from * around, join, ch 1. (20 sts)

Round 21: Sc in each st around, join, ch 1.

At this point attach the safety eyes between rounds 8 and 9 (about 8 sts apart). Then stuff before closing the head.

Round 22: Sc2tog around, join, ch 1. (10 sts)

Round 23: Sc2tog around, join. (5 sts)

Fasten off leaving a long tail.

Use long tail to close final round and weave in ends.

Body:

With Sky yarn, create a magic ring, ch 1 and make 10 sc in ring, join to first sc, ch 1.

Round 2: 2 sc in each st around, join, ch 1. (20 sts)

Round 3: *2 sc in next st, sc in next st, repeat from * around, join, ch 1. (30 sts)

Round 4: Sc in each st around, join, ch 1.

Round 5: *2 sc in next st, sc in next 2 sts, repeat from * around, join, ch 1. (40 sts)

Round 6: Sc in each st around, join, ch 1.

Round 7: *2 sc in next st, sc in next 3 sts, repeat from * around, join, ch 1. (50 sts)

Rounds 8–19: Sc in each st around, join, ch 1.
Stuff and continue to stuff as you go.

Round 20: *Sc2tog, sc in next 3 sts, repeat from * around, join, ch 1. (40 sts)

Rounds 21–22: Sc in each st around, join, ch 1.

Round 23: *Sc2tog, sc in next 2 sts, repeat from * around, join, ch 1. (30 sts)

Rounds 24–25: Sc in each st around, join, ch 1.

Round 26: *Sc2tog, sc in next st, repeat from * around, join, ch 1. (20 sts)

Rounds 27–35: Sc in each st around, join, ch 1.

Round 36: *Sc2tog, sc in next 2 sts, repeat from * around, join, ch 1. (15 sts)

Rounds 37–38: Sc in each st around, join, ch 1.
Fasten off leaving a long strand of yarn and stuff. Use long strand to close final round and sew on head.

Belly:

With Bright Yellow yarn, ch 11, sc in second ch from hook and the remaining 9 chs, ch 1, turn. (10 sts)

Row 2: 2 sc in first st, sc in next 8 sts, 2 sc in last st, ch 1, turn. (12 sts)

Rows 3–6: Sc in each st across, ch 1, turn.

Row 7: Sc2tog, sc in next 8 sts, sc2tog over last 2 sts, ch 1, turn. (10 sts)

Row 8: Sc in each st across, ch 1, turn.

Row 9: Sc2tog, sc in next 6 sts, sc2tog over last 2 sts, ch 1, turn. (8 sts)

Rows 10–13: Sc in each st across, ch 1, turn.

Row 14: Sc2tog, sc in next 4 sts, sc2tog over last 2 sts, ch 1, turn. (6 sts)

Row 15: Sc2tog, sc in next 2 sts, sc2tog over last 2 sts, ch 1, turn. (4 sts)

Rows 16–29: Sc in each st across, ch 1, turn.

Row 30: Sc2tog twice, then continue to sc around all edges of the belly piece, join to first sc. Fasten off leaving a long tail and sew onto belly area of body.

Wings (make 2):

With Sky yarn, create a magic ring, ch 1 and make 6 sc in ring, join to first sc, ch 1.

Round 2: *2 sc in next st, sc in next st, repeat from * around, join, ch 1. (9 sts)

Round 3: Sc in each st around, join, ch 1.

Round 4: *2 sc in next st, sc in next 2 sts, repeat from * around, join, ch 1. (12 sts)

Round 5: Sc in each st around, join, ch 1.

Round 6: *2 sc in next st, sc in next 2 sts, repeat from * around, join, ch 1. (16 sts)

Round 7: Sc in each st around, join, ch 1.

Round 8: *2 sc in next st, sc in next 3 sts, repeat from * around, join, ch 1. (20 sts)

Round 9: Sc in each st around, join, ch 1.

Round 10: *2 sc in next st, sc in next 4 sts, repeat from * around, join, ch 1. (24 sts)

Round 11: *2 sc in next st, sc in next 5 sts, repeat from * around, join, ch 1. (28 sts)

Rounds 12–15: Sc in each st around, join, ch 1.

Round 16: *Sc2tog, sc in next 2 sts, repeat from * around, join, ch 1. (21 sts)

Round 17: Sc in each st around, join, ch 1.

Round 18: *Sc2tog, sc in next st, repeat from *
    around, join, ch 1. (14 sts)

Rounds 19–21: Sc in each st around, join, ch 1.

Fasten off leaving a long tail.

Wings should be unstuffed and lay flat.

Use long tail to sew the top closed and attach
    where head and body meet.

Beak (make 2 pieces):

With Bright Yellow yarn, create a magic ring, make 4
    sc in ring, join to first sc, ch 1.

Round 2: 2 sc in each st around, join, ch 1. (8 sts)

Round 3: Sc in each st around, join, ch 1.

Round 4: *2 sc in next st, sc in next st, repeat from *
    around, join, ch 1. (12 sts)

Round 5: Sc in each st around, join, ch 1.

Round 6: *2 sc in next st, sc in next 2 sts, join,
    ch 1. (16 sts)

Round 7: Sc in each st around, join.

Fasten off leaving a long tail, leaving beak pieces
    unstuffed.

Use long tail to sew onto head about 3 rows down
    from the eyes. Beak pieces should be sewn on to
    look like an open mouth.

OSWALD THE *Owl*

Whooo doesn't love owls? Stitch up Oswald the Owl in a variety of colors! He's the perfect amigurumi for all ages. You can even make a family of owls for your home décor—they would be adorable perched atop a mantel.

Size: 11 inches tall x 6 inches wide

Materials:
- Bernat Super Value Yarn in Oatmeal (light brown)
- Bernat Super Value Yarn in Taupe (dark brown)
- Bernat Super Value Yarn in Pumpkin
- Size H Crochet Hook
- 12mm Safety Eyes
- Poly-fil Fiber Stuffing
- Tapestry Needle

Body:

With Oatmeal yarn, create a magic ring, ch 1 and make 10 sc in ring, join to first sc, ch 1.

Round 2: 2 sc in each st around, join, ch 1. (20 sts)

Round 3: *2 sc in next st, sc in next st, repeat from * around, join, ch 1. (30 sts)

Round 4: Sc in each st around, join, ch 1.

Round 5: *2 sc in next st, sc in next 2 sts, repeat from * around, join, ch 1. (40 sts)

Round 6: Sc in each st around, join, ch 1.

Round 7: *2 sc in next st, sc in next 3 sts, repeat from * around, join, ch 1. (50 sts)

Rounds 8–19: Sc in each st around, join, ch 1.

Round 20: *Sc2tog, sc in next 3 sts, repeat from * around, join, ch 1. (40 sts)

Rounds 21–22: Sc in each st around, join, ch 1.

Round 23: *Sc2tog, sc in next 2 sts, repeat from * around, join, ch 1. (30 sts)

Rounds 24–25: Sc in each st around, join, ch 1.

Round 26: *Sc2tog, sc in next st, repeat from * around, join, ch 1. (20 sts)

Rounds 27–28: Sc in each st around, join, ch 1.

Round 29: Sc2tog around, join. (10 sts)

Fasten off leaving a long tail and stuff, leaving top open.

Head:

With Taupe yarn, create a magic ring, ch 1 and make 10 sc in ring, join to first sc, ch 1.

Round 2: 2 sc in each st around, join, ch 1. (20 sts)

Round 3: Sc in each st around, join, ch 1.

Round 4: *2 sc in next st, sc in next st, repeat from * around, join, ch 1. (30 sts)

Round 5: Sc in each st around, join, ch 1.

Round 6: *2 sc in next st, sc in next 2 sts, repeat from * around, join, ch 1. (40 sts)

Round 7: *2 sc in next st, sc in next 3 sts, repeat from * around, join, ch 1. (50 sts)

Rounds 8–15: Sc in each st around, join, ch 1.

Round 16: *Sc2tog, sc in next 3 sts, repeat from * around, join, ch 1. (40 sts)

Round 17: Sc in each st around, join, ch 1.

Round 18: *Sc2tog, sc in next 2 sts, repeat from * around, join, ch 1. (30 sts)

Round 19: Sc in each st around, join, ch 1.

Fasten off leaving a long tail.

Pinch the top so it's closed flat. Use long tail to sew top edges together. The ears will automatically take shape when you sew the top closed. Then stuff firmly.

Eyes (make 2):

With Oatmeal yarn, create a magic ring, ch 1 and make 10 sc in ring, join to first sc, ch 1.

Round 2: 2 sc in each st around, join, ch 1. (20 sts)

Round 3: *2 sc in next st, sc in next st, repeat from * around, join. (30 sts)

Fasten off leaving a long tail.

Add safety eyes slightly off-center and sew onto front of head so both eyes touch in the middle.

Beak:

With Pumpkin yarn, ch 4, sc in second ch from hook, hdc in next ch, dc in last ch, fasten off leaving a long tail.

Sew beak onto head so it overlaps the bottom of eyes.

Wings (make 2):

With Taupe yarn, create a magic ring, ch 1 and make 6 sc in ring, join to first sc, ch 1.

Round 2: *2 sc in next st, sc in next st, repeat from * around, join, ch 1. (9 sts)

Round 3: Sc in each st around, join, ch 1.

Round 4: *2 sc in next st, sc in next 2 sts, repeat from * around, join, ch 1. (12 sts)

Round 5: Sc in each st around, join, ch 1.

Round 6: *2 sc in next st, sc in next 2 sts, repeat from * around, join, ch 1. (16 sts)

Round 7: Sc in each st around, join, ch 1.

Round 8: *2 sc in next st, sc in next 3 sts, repeat from * around, join, ch 1. (20 sts)

Round 9: Sc in each st around, join, ch 1.

Round 10: *2 sc in next st, sc in next 4 sts, repeat from * around, join, ch 1. (24 sts)

Round 11: *2 sc in next st, sc in next 5 sts, repeat from * around, join, ch 1. (28 sts)

Rounds 12–15: Sc in each st around, join, ch 1.

Round 16: *Sc2tog, sc in next 2 sts, repeat from * around, join, ch 1. (21 sts)

Round 17: Sc in each st around, join, ch 1.

Round 18: *Sc2tog, sc in next st, repeat from * around, join, ch 1. (14 sts)

Rounds 19–21: Sc in each st around, join, ch 1.

Fasten off leaving a long tail.

Wings should be unstuffed and lay flat.

Use long tail to sew the top closed and attach where head and body meet.

Feet (make 2):

With Pumpkin yarn, create a magic ring, ch 1 and
make 10 sc in ring, join to first sc, ch 1.

Round 2: 2 sc in each st around, join, ch 1. (20 sts)

Rounds 3–7: Sc in each st around, join, ch 1.

Round 8: *Sc2tog, sc in next 3 sts, repeat from *
around, join. (16 sts)

Fasten off leaving a long tail.

Stuff lightly and pinch opening flat. Use long tail
to sew on bottom of body so stuffed foot ends
stick out.

PENELOPE THE *Penguin*

Penelope the Penguin will waddle her way right into your heart! She is a sweet little baby and her solid gray body and simple eye construction make for easy stitching. You may have a whole group of penguins crocheted before you know it!

Size: 10 inches tall x 8 inches wide

Materials:
- Bernat Super Value Yarn in Soft Gray
- Bernat Super Value Yarn in Black
- Bernat Super Value Yarn in White
- Bernat Super Value Yarn in Bright Yellow
- Size H Crochet Hook
- 12mm Safety Eyes
- Poly-fil Fiber Stuffing
- Tapestry Needle

Body:

With Soft Gray yarn, create a magic ring, ch 1 and make 10 sc in ring, join to first sc, ch 1.

Round 2: 2 sc in each st around, join, ch 1. (20 sts)

Round 3: *2 sc in next st, sc in next st, repeat from * around, join, ch 1. (30 sts)

Round 4: Sc in each st around, join, ch 1.

Round 5: *2 sc in next st, sc in next 2 sts, repeat from * around, join, ch 1. (40 sts)

Round 6: Sc in each st around, join, ch 1.

Round 7: *2 sc in next st, sc in next 3 sts, repeat from * around, join, ch 1. (50 sts)

Rounds 8–19: Sc in each st around, join, ch 1.

Round 20: *Sc2tog, sc in next 3 sts, repeat from * around, join, ch 1. (40 sts)

Rounds 21–22: Sc in each st around, join, ch 1.

Round 23: *Sc2tog, sc in next 2 sts, repeat from * around, join, ch 1. (30 sts)

Rounds 24–25: Sc in each st around, join, ch 1.

Round 26: *Sc2tog, sc in next st, repeat from * around, join, ch 1. (20 sts)

Rounds 27–28: Sc in each st around, join, ch 1.

Round 29: Sc2tog around, join. (10 sts)

Fasten off leaving a long tail and stuff, leaving top open.

Head:

With Black yarn, create a magic ring, ch 1 and make 10 sc in ring, join to first sc, ch 1.

Round 2: 2 sc in each st around, join, ch 1. (20 sts)

Round 3: Sc in each st around, join, ch 1.

Round 4: *2 sc in next st, sc in next st, repeat from * around, join, ch 1. (30 sts)

Round 5: Sc in each st around, join, ch 1.

Round 6: *2 sc in next st, sc in next 2 sts, repeat from * around, join, ch 1. (40 sts)

Round 7: *2 sc in next st, sc in next 3 sts, repeat from * around, join, ch 1. (50 sts)

Rounds 8–15: Sc in each st around, join, ch 1.

Round 16: *Sc2tog, sc in next 3 sts, repeat from * around, join, ch 1. (40 sts)

Round 17: Sc in each st around, join, ch 1.

Round 18: *Sc2tog, sc in next 2 sts, repeat from * around, join, ch 1. (30 sts)

Round 19: Sc in each st around, join, ch 1.

Round 20: *Sc2tog, sc in next st, repeat from * around, join, ch 1. (20 sts)

Round 21: Sc in each st around, join, ch 1.

At this point stuff before closing the head.

Round 22: Sc2tog around, join, ch 1. (10 sts)

Round 23: Sc2tog around, join. (5 sts)

Fasten off leaving a long tail.

Use long tail to close final round and weave in ends.

Use long tail of body to sew on head.

Eye Patches (make 2):

With White yarn, ch 7, sc in second ch from hook and in next 4 chs, 4 sc in last ch.

Now working on other side of ch, sc in first 5 chs, 4 sc in last ch, join, ch 2. (18 sts)

Round 2: *2 dc in first st, dc in next st, repeat from * around until you have 2 sts left unworked, sc in last 2 sts and join to first dc. (28 sts)

Fasten off leaving a long tail.

The part with the 2 sc sts is the bottom. Add safety eyes to middle of eye patches and then sew onto head.

Sew onto front of head. About 8 rows from the top.

Beak:

With Bright Yellow yarn ch 3, sc in second ch from hook, 2 sc in last ch.

Now working on other side of ch, sc in first ch, 2 sc in last ch, join, ch 1. (6 sts)

Round 2: *2 sc in next st, sc in next st, repeat from * around, join, ch 1. (9 sts)

Round 3: Sc in each st around, join.

Fasten off leaving a long tail.

Sew to head overlapping bottom of eye patches.

Wings (make 2):

With Black yarn, create a magic ring, ch 1 and make 6 sc in ring, join to first sc, ch 1.

Round 2: *2 sc in next st, sc in next st, repeat from * around, join, ch 1. (9 sts)

Round 3: Sc in each st around, join, ch 1.

Round 4: *2 sc in next st, sc in next 2 sts, repeat from * around, join, ch 1. (12 sts)

Round 5: Sc in each st around, join, ch 1.

Round 6: *2 sc in next st, sc in next 2 sts, repeat from * around, join, ch 1. (16 sts)

Round 7: Sc in each st around, join, ch 1.

Round 8: *2 sc in next st, sc in next 3 sts, repeat from * around, join, ch 1. (20 sts)

Round 9: Sc in each st around, join, ch 1.

Round 10: *2 sc in next st, sc in next 4 sts, repeat from * around, join, ch 1. (24 sts)

Round 11: *2 sc in next st, sc in next 5 sts, repeat from * around, join, ch 1. (28 sts)

Rounds 12–15: Sc in each st around, join, ch 1.

Round 16: *Sc2tog, sc in next 2 sts, repeat from * around, join, ch 1. (21 sts)

Round 17: Sc in each st around, join, ch 1.

Round 18: *Sc2tog, sc in next st, repeat from * around, join, ch 1. (14 sts)

Rounds 19–21: Sc in each st around, join, ch 1.

Fasten off leaving a long tail.

Wings should be unstuffed and lay flat.

Use long tail to sew the top closed and attach where head and body meet.

Feet (make 2):

With Bright Yellow yarn, create a magic ring, ch 1 and make 10 sc in ring, join to first sc, ch 1.

Round 2: 2 sc in each st around, join, ch 1. (20 sts)

Rounds 3–7: Sc in each st around, join, ch 1.

Round 8: *Sc2tog, sc in next 3 sts, repeat from * around, join. (16 sts)

Fasten off leaving a long tail.

Stuff lightly and pinch opening flat. Use long tail to sew on bottom of body so stuffed foot ends stick out.

QUINN THE *Queen Bee*

She's the queen of the colony and wears her crown well. Her stinger is soft and body is plush. Get busy with this Queen Bee pattern!

Size: 14 inches tall x 8 inches wide

Materials:

- Bernat Super Value Yarn in Bright Yellow
- Bernat Super Value Yarn in Black
- Bernat Super Value Yarn in White
- Bernat Super Value Yarn in Berry (small amount, optional for crown and smile)
- Size H Crochet Hook
- 12mm Safety Eyes
- Poly-fil Fiber Stuffing
- Tapestry Needle

Body:

Start with Bright Yellow yarn, then alternate between Black and Bright Yellow every 4 rounds.

With Bright Yellow yarn, create a magic ring, ch 1 and make 10 sc in ring, join to first sc, ch 1.

Round 2: 2 sc in each st around, join, ch 1. (20 sts)

Round 3: *2 sc in next st, sc in next st, repeat from * around, join, ch 1. (30 sts)

Round 4: Sc in each st around, join, ch 1.

Round 5: *2 sc in next st, sc in next 2 sts, repeat from * around, join, ch 1. (40 sts)

Round 6: Sc in each st around, join, ch 1.

Round 7: *2 sc in next st, sc in next 3 sts, repeat from * around, join, ch 1. (50 sts)

Rounds 8–19: Sc in each st around, join, ch 1.

Round 20: *Sc2tog, sc in next 3 sts, repeat from * around, join, ch 1. (40 sts)

Rounds 21–22: Sc in each st around, join, ch 1.

Round 23: *Sc2tog, sc in next 2 sts, repeat from * around, join, ch 1. (30 sts)

Rounds 24–25: Sc in each st around, join, ch 1.

Round 26: *Sc2tog, sc in next st, repeat from * around, join, ch 1. (20 sts)

Rounds 27–28: Sc in each st around, join, ch 1.

At this point stuff before closing body.

Round 29: Sc2tog around, join, ch 1. (10 sts)

Rounds 30–31: Sc in each st around, join, ch 1.

Round 32: Sc2tog around, join. (5 sts)

Fasten off leaving a long tail.

Use long tail to close final round and weave in ends.

Head:

With Bright Yellow yarn, create a magic ring, ch 1 and make 10 sc in ring, join to first sc, ch 1.

Round 2: 2 sc in each st around, join, ch 1. (20 sts)

Round 3: Sc in each st around, join, ch 1.

Round 4: *2 sc in next st, sc in next st, repeat from * around, join, ch 1. (30 sts)

Round 5: Sc in each st around, join, ch 1.

Round 6: *2 sc in next st, sc in next 2 sts, repeat from * around, join, ch 1. (40 sts)

Round 7: *2 sc in next st, sc in next 3 sts, repeat from * around, join, ch 1. (50 sts)

Rounds 8–15: Sc in each st around, join, ch 1.

Round 16: *Sc2tog, sc in next 3 sts, repeat from * around, join, ch 1. (40 sts)

Round 17: Sc in each st around, join, ch 1.

Round 18: *Sc2tog, sc in next 2 sts, repeat from * around, join, ch 1. (30 sts)

Round 19: Sc in each st around, join, ch 1.

Round 20: *Sc2tog, sc in next st, repeat from * around, join, ch 1. (20 sts)

Round 21: Sc in each st around, join, ch 1.

At this point stitch on the mouth and add safety eyes. Then stuff before closing the head. Using red yarn and your tapestry needle, stitch on a small "v" for the mouth in the middle of the head, 14 rows down from the top. Add safety eyes 2 rows above the mouth.

Round 22: Sc2tog around, join, ch 1. (10 sts)

Round 23: Sc2tog around, join. (5 sts)

Fasten off leaving a long tail.

Use long tail to close final round and sew to top of body, stinger pointed down.

Bee Wings:

Large Part of Wing (make 2):

With White yarn, create a magic ring, ch 1 and make 10 sc in ring, join to first sc, ch 1.

Round 2: 2 sc in each st around, join, ch 1. (20 sts)

Rounds 3–7: Sc in each st around, join, ch 1.

Round 8: Sc2tog, sc in next 3 sts, repeat from * around, join. (16 sts)

Fasten off leaving a long tail.

Small Part of Wing (make 2):

With White yarn, create a magic ring, ch 1 and make 6 sc in ring, join to first sc, ch 1.

Round 2: 2 sc in each st around, join, ch 1. (12 sts)

Rounds 3–6: Sc in each st around, join, ch 1.

Fasten off leaving a long tail.

Stuff each part lightly. Use long tails to sew one large wing and one small wing to each side of body.

Antennae (make 2):

With Black yarn, create a magic ring, ch 1 and make 6 sc in ring, join to first sc, ch 1.

Round 2: *2 sc in next st, sc in next st, repeat from * around, join, ch 1. (9 sts)

Round 3: *2 sc in next st, sc in next 2 sts, repeat from * around, join, ch 1. (12 sts)

Round 4: Sc in each st around, join, ch 1.

Round 5: *Sc2tog, sc in next 2 sts, repeat from * around, join, ch 1. (9 sts)

Round 6: *Sc2tog, sc in next st, repeat from * around, join, ch 1. (6 sts)

At this point stuff the "ball" then continue.

Rounds 7–10: Sc in each st around, join, ch 1.

Fasten off leaving a long tail and sew onto top of head.

Crown:

With Berry yarn, ch 11, sc in second ch from hook, sc in next ch, ch 2 and sc in second ch from hook, sc in next ch, skip a ch, dc in next ch, ch 2 and sc + dc in second ch from hook, skip a ch, sc in next ch, ch 2 and sc in second ch from hook, sc in last 3 chs.

Fasten off leaving a long tail and sew to top of head, between and slightly in front of antennae.

ROSY THE *Rabbit*

Rosy the Rabbit is pretty and pink and as sweet as can be! This beautiful bunny can be stitched up in any color, and with minimal embellishments, it's a simple pattern that will please all.

Size: 10 inches tall x 8 inches wide

Materials:

- Bernat Super Value Yarn in Baby Pink
- Bernat Super Value Yarn in White
- Size H Crochet Hook
- 12mm Safety Eyes
- Poly-fil Fiber Stuffing
- Tapestry Needle
- Pom-Pom Maker (optional, for making tail)

Body:

With Baby Pink yarn, create a magic ring, ch 1 and make 10 sc in ring, join to first sc, ch 1.

Round 2: 2 sc in each st around, join, ch 1. (20 sts)

Round 3: 2 sc in next st, sc in next st, repeat from * around, join, ch 1. (30 sts)

Round 4: Sc in each st around, join, ch 1.

Round 5: *2 sc in next st, sc in next 2 sts, repeat from * around, join, ch 1. (40 sts)

Round 6: Sc in each st around, join, ch 1.

Round 7: *2 sc in next st, sc in next 3 sts, repeat from * around, join, ch 1. (50 sts)

Rounds 8–19: Sc in each st around, join, ch 1.

Round 20: *Sc2tog, sc in next 3 sts, repeat from * around, join, ch 1. (40 sts)

Rounds 21–22: Sc in each st around, join, ch 1.

Round 23: *Sc2tog, sc in next 2 sts, repeat from * around, join, ch 1. (30 sts)

Rounds 24–25: Sc in each st around, join, ch 1.

Round 26: *Sc2tog, sc in next st, repeat from * around, join, ch 1. (20 sts)

Rounds 27–28: Sc in each st around, join, ch 1.

Round 29: *Sc2tog around, join. (10 sts)

Fasten off leaving a long tail and stuff, leaving top open.

Head:

With Baby Pink yarn, create a magic ring, ch 1 and make 10 sc in ring, join to first sc, ch 1.

Round 2: 2 sc in each st around, join, ch 1. (20 sts)

Round 3: Sc in each st around, join, ch 1.

Round 4: *2 sc in next st, sc in next st, repeat from * around, join, ch 1. (30 sts)

Round 5: Sc in each st around, join, ch 1.

Round 6: *2 sc in next st, sc in next 2 sts, repeat from * around, join, ch 1. (40 sts)

Round 7: *2 sc in next st, sc in next 3 sts, repeat from * around, join, ch 1. (50 sts)

Rounds 8–15: Sc in each st around, join, ch 1.

Round 16: *Sc2tog, sc in next 3 sts, repeat from *
   around, join, ch 1. (40 sts)

Round 17: Sc in each st around, join, ch 1.

Round 18: *Sc2tog, sc in next 2 sts, repeat from *
   around, join, ch 1. (30 sts)

Round 19: Sc in each st around, join, ch 1.

Round 20: *Sc2tog, sc in next st, repeat from *
   around, join, ch 1. (20 sts)

Round 21: Sc in each st around, join, ch 1.

*At this point attach the safety eyes and stitch on
a triangle nose and little mouth with White yarn.
Then stuff before closing the head.*

Round 22: Sc2tog around, join, ch 1. (10 sts)

Round 23: Sc2tog around, join. (5 sts)

Fasten off leaving a long tail.

Use long tail to close final round and weave in ends.

Use long tail of body to sew on head.

Legs (make 2):

With White yarn, create a magic ring, ch 1 and make
   6 sc in ring, join to first sc, ch 1.

Round 2: 2 sc in each st around, join, ch 2. (12 sts)

Round 3: 2 dc in first 3 sts, 2 hdc in next 2 sts, 2 sc in
   next 5 sts, 2 hdc in last 2 sts, join, *change to Baby
   Pink yarn*, ch 1. (24 sts)

Round 4: Working in back loops only for this round,
   sc in each st around, join, ch 1.

Rounds 5–6: Sc in each st around, join, ch 1.

Round 7: Sc2tog 6 times, sc in remaining 12 sts, join,
   ch 1. (18 sts)

Round 8: Sc in each st around, join, ch 1.

Round 9: Sc2tog 5 times, sc in remaining 8 sts, join,
   ch 1. (13 sts)

Rounds 10–14: Sc in each st around, join, ch 1.

Fasten off leaving a long tail and stuff.

Use long tail to sew onto bottom of body.

Arms (make 2):

With Baby Pink yarn, create a magic ring, ch 1 and
   make 10 sc in ring, join to first sc, ch 1.

Round 2: *2 sc in next st, sc in next st, repeat from *
   around, join, ch 1. (15 sts)

Rounds 3–4: Sc in each st around, join, ch 1.

Round 5: *Sc2tog, sc in next 3 sts, repeat from *
   around, join, ch 1. (12 sts)

Rounds 6–22: Sc in each st around, join, ch 1.

Fasten off leaving a long tail and stuff.

Flatten opening and use long tail to sew onto body
   under the head.

Ears (make 2):

With Baby Pink yarn, create a magic ring, ch 1 and
   make 10 sc in ring, join to first sc, ch 1.

Round 2: 2 sc in each st around, join, ch 1. (20 sts)

Round 3: Sc in each st around, join, ch 1.

Round 4: *2 sc in next st, sc in next 3 sts, repeat
   from * around, join, ch 1. (25 sts)

Rounds 5–9: Sc in each st around, join, ch 1.

Round 10: *Sc2tog, sc in next 3 sts, repeat from *
   around, join, ch 1. (20 sts)

Rounds 11–12: Sc in each st around, join, ch 1.

Round 13: *Sc2tog, sc in next 2 sts, repeat from *
   around, join, ch 1. (15 sts)

Rounds 14–15: Sc in each st around, join, ch 1.

Round 16: *Sc2tog, sc in next st, repeat from *
   around, join, ch 1. (10 sts)

Rounds 17–23: Sc in each st around, join, ch 1.

Fasten off leaving a long tail.

Ears should be unstuffed and lay flat.

Use long tail to sew ears onto top of head, about 3 rounds from top.

Tail:

With White yarn, make a small pom-pom using pom-pom maker or other method. Sew onto bottom back of body.

SAMMY THE *Snail*

Snails are known to be slow but when you are working with a crochet pattern made up of simple stitches things go quickly! Speed through this amigurumi pattern that consists of a repetition of single crochet stitches and you will have a seriously cute snail in no time at all!

Size: 10 inches wide x 8 inches tall

Materials:

- Bernat Super Value Yarn in Pumpkin
- Bernat Super Value Yarn in Oatmeal
- Size H Crochet Hook
- 12mm Safety Eyes
- Poly-fil Fiber Stuffing
- Tapestry Needle

Shell:

With Pumpkin yarn, create a magic ring, ch 1 and make 10 sc in ring, join to first sc, ch 1.

Round 2: 2 sc in each st around, join, ch 1. (20 sts)

Rounds 3–65: Sc in each st around, join, ch 1.

Fasten off leaving a long tail.

Stuff lightly, leaving last 10 rounds unstuffed, and roll up.

Use long tail to sew together so it stays rolled.

Head and Body:

With Oatmeal yarn, create a magic ring, ch 1 and make 10 sc in ring, join to first sc, ch 1.

Round 2: 2 sc in each st around, join, ch 1. (20 sts)

Round 3: Sc in each st around, join, ch 1.

Round 4: *2 sc in next st, sc in next st, repeat from * around, join, ch 1. (30 sts)

Round 5: Sc in each st around, join, ch 1.

Round 6: *2 sc in next st, sc in next 2 sts, repeat from * around, join, ch 1. (40 sts)

Round 7: *2 sc in next st, sc in next 3 sts, repeat from * around, join, ch 1. (50 sts)

Rounds 8–15: Sc in each st around, join, ch 1.

Round 16: *Sc2tog, sc in next 3 sts, repeat from * around, join, ch 1. (40 sts)

Round 17: Sc in each st around, join, ch 1.

Round 18: *Sc2tog, sc in next 2 sts, repeat from * around, join, ch 1. (30 sts)

Round 19: Sc in each st around, join, ch 1.

Round 20: *Sc2tog, sc in next st, repeat from * around, join, ch 1. (20 sts)

At this point attach the safety eyes. Then stuff the head and continue as you go, stuffing the head firmly and lightly stuffing the skinny body portion.

Rounds 21–50: Sc in each st around, join, ch 1.

Round 51: *Sc2tog, sc in next 3 sts, repeat from * around, join, ch 1. (16 sts)

Round 52: Sc in each st around, join, ch 1.

Round 53: *Sc2tog, sc in next 2 sts, repeat from * around, join, ch 1. (12 sts)

Round 54: Sc in each st around, join, ch 1.

Round 55: *Sc2tog, sc in next 2 sts, repeat from * around, join, ch 1. (9 sts)

Round 56: Sc in each st around, join, ch 1.

Round 57: Sc2tog around to last st, sc in last st. Join. (5 sts)

Fasten off leaving a long tail.

Use long tail to close final round and weave in ends.

Use some extra yarn to attach shell to head and body, pulling head into upright position.

Antennae (make 2):

With Oatmeal yarn, create a magic ring, ch 1 and make 6 sc in ring, join to first sc, ch 1.

Round 2: *2 sc in next st, sc in next st, repeat from * around, join, ch 1. (9 sts)

Round 3: *2 sc in next st, sc in next 2 sts, repeat from * around, join, ch 1. (12 sts)

Round 4: Sc in each st around, join, ch 1.

Round 5: *Sc2tog, sc in next 2 sts, repeat from * around, join, ch 1. (9 sts)

Round 6: *Sc2tog, sc in next st, repeat from * around, join, ch 1. (6 sts)

At this point stuff the "ball," then continue.

Rounds 7–10: Sc in each st around, join, ch 1.

Fasten off leaving a long tail and sew onto top of head.

TINA THE *Turtle*

Tina is a snap to stitch, not slow and steady like other turtles. With simple stitches and a pattern that repeats, you can crochet Tina the Turtle in no time at all!

Size: 12 inches wide x 6 inches tall

Materials:

- Bernat Super Value Yarn in Soft Fern (light green)
- Bernat Super Value Yarn in Lush (dark green)
- Size H Crochet Hook
- 12mm Safety Eyes
- Poly-fil Fiber Stuffing
- Tapestry Needle

Body (Shell) Pattern:

Bottom of Shell:

With Soft Fern yarn, create a magic ring, ch 1 and make 10 sc in ring, join to first sc, ch 1.

Round 2: 2 sc in each st around, join, ch 1. (20 sts)

Round 3: *2 sc in next st, sc in next st, repeat from * around, join, ch 1. (30 sts)

Round 4: Sc in each st around, join, ch 1.

Round 5: *2 sc in next st, sc in next 2 sts, repeat from * around, join, ch 1. (40 sts)

Round 6: Sc in each st around, join, ch 1.

Round 7: *2 sc in next st, sc in next 3 sts, repeat from * around, join, ch 1. (50 sts)

Rounds 8–11: Sc in each st around, join, ch 1.

Fasten off and weave in ends.

Top of Shell:

With Lush yarn, create a magic ring, ch 1 and make 10 sc in ring, join to first sc, ch 1.

Round 2: 2 sc in each st around, join, ch 1. (20 sts)

Round 3: *2 sc in next st, sc in next st, repeat from * around, join, ch 1. (30 sts)

Round 4: Sc in each st around, join, ch 1.

Round 5: *2 sc in next st, sc in next 2 sts, repeat from * around, join, ch 1. (40 sts)

Round 6: Sc in each st around, join, ch 1.

Round 7: *2 sc in next st, sc in next 3 sts, repeat from * around, join, ch 1. (50 sts)

Rounds 8–13: Sc in each st around, join, ch 1.

Do NOT fasten off.

Place top and bottom of shell together and use the Lush yarn to sc the two pieces together. Stuff before closing.

Head:

With Soft Fern yarn, create a magic ring, ch 1 and make 10 sc in ring, join to first sc, ch 1.

Round 2: 2 sc in each st around, join, ch 1. (20 sts)

Round 3: Sc in each st around, join, ch 1.

Round 4: *2 sc in next st, sc in next st, repeat from * around, join, ch 1. (30 sts)

Round 5: Sc in each st around, join, ch 1.

Round 6: *2 sc in next st, sc in next 2 sts, repeat from * around, join, ch 1. (40 sts)

Round 7: *2 sc in next st, sc in next 3 sts, repeat from * around, join, ch 1. (50 sts)

Rounds 8–15: Sc in each st around, join, ch 1.

Round 16: *Sc2tog, sc in next 3 sts, repeat from * around, join, ch 1. (40 sts)

Round 17: Sc in each st around, join, ch 1.

Round 18: *Sc2tog, sc in next 2 sts, repeat from * around, join, ch 1. (30 sts)

Round 19: Sc in each st around, join, ch 1.

Round 20: *Sc2tog, sc in next st, repeat from * around, join, ch 1. (20 sts)

Round 21: Sc in each st around, join, ch 1.

At this point attach the safety eyes. Then stuff before closing the head.

Round 22: Sc2tog around, join, ch 1. (10 sts)

Round 23: Sc2tog around, join. (5 sts)

Fasten off leaving a long tail.

Use long tail to close final round and to sew head onto shell.

Legs (make 4):

With Soft Fern yarn, create a magic ring, ch 1 and make 10 sc in ring, join to first sc, ch 1.

Round 2: 2 sc in each st around, join, ch 1. (20 sts)

Rounds 3–7: Sc in each st around, join, ch 1.

Round 8: *Sc2tog, sc in next 3 sts, repeat from * around, join. (16 sts)

Fasten off leaving a long tail.

Stuff and use long tail to sew legs onto shell.

Tail:

With Soft Fern yarn, create a magic ring, ch 1 and make 4 sc in ring, join, ch 1.

Round 2: *2 sc in next st, sc in next st, repeat from * around, join, ch 1. (6 sts)

Round 3: Sc in each st around, join, ch 1.

Round 4: *2 sc in next st, sc in next 2 sts, repeat from * around, join, ch 1. (8 sts)

Round 5: Sc in each st around, join, ch 1.

Round 6: *2 sc in next st, sc in next 3 sts, repeat from * around, join, ch 1. (10 sts)

Rounds 7–8: Sc in each st around, join, ch 1.

Fasten off leaving a long tail and sew onto back of shell.

UNIQUA THE *Unicorn*

The most magical creature of the bunch is ready for you to stitch up! With a rainbow coil mane, Uniqua the Unicorn will be loved and requested by all! Plan on crocheting lots of these as gifts.

Size: 10 inches tall x 8 inches wide

Materials:

- Bernat Super Value Yarn in White
- Bernat Super Value Yarn in Baby Pink
- Bernat Super Value Yarn in Soft Fern
- Bernat Super Value Yarn in Lilac
- Bernat Super Value Yarn in Bright Yellow
- Size H Crochet Hook
- 12mm Safety Eyes
- Poly-fil Fiber Stuffing
- Tapestry Needle
- Removable Stitch Marker (optional)

Body:

With White yarn, create a magic ring, ch 1 and make 10 sc in ring, join to first sc, ch 1.

Round 2: 2 sc in each st around, join, ch 1. (20 sts)

Round 3: *2 sc in next st, sc in next st, repeat from * around, join, ch 1. (30 sts)

Round 4: Sc in each st around, join, ch 1.

Round 5: *2 sc in next st, sc in next 2 sts, repeat from * around, join, ch 1. (40 sts)

Round 6: Sc in each st around, join, ch 1.

Round 7: *2 sc in next st, sc in next 3 sts, repeat from * around, join, ch 1. (50 sts)

Rounds 8–19: Sc in each st around, join, ch 1.

Round 20: *Sc2tog, sc in next 3 sts, repeat from * around, join, ch 1. (40 sts)

Rounds 21–22: Sc in each st around, join, ch 1.

Round 23: *Sc2tog, sc in next 2 sts, repeat from * around, join, ch 1. (30 sts)

Rounds 24–25: Sc in each st around, join, ch 1.

Round 26: *Sc2tog, sc in next st, repeat from * around, join, ch 1. (20 sts)

Rounds 27–28: Sc in each st around, join, ch 1.

Round 29: Sc2tog around, join. (10 sts)

Fasten off leaving a long tail and stuff, leaving top open.

Head:

With White yarn, create a magic ring, ch 1 and make 10 sc in ring, join to first sc, ch 1.

Round 2: 2 sc in each st around, join, ch 1. (20 sts)

Round 3: Sc in each st around, join, ch 1.

Round 4: *2 sc in next st, sc in next st, repeat from * around, join, ch 1. (30 sts)

Round 5: Sc in each st around, join, ch 1.

Round 6: *2 sc in next st, sc in next 2 sts, repeat from * around, join, ch 1. (40 sts)

Round 7: *2 sc in next st, sc in next 3 sts, repeat from * around, join, ch 1. (50 sts)

Rounds 8–15: Sc in each st around, join, ch 1.

Round 16: *Sc2tog, sc in next 3 sts, repeat from * around, join, ch 1. (40 sts)

Round 17: Sc in each st around, join, ch 1.

Round 18: *Sc2tog, sc in next 2 sts, repeat from * around, join, ch 1. (30 sts)

Round 19: Sc in each st around, join, ch 1.

Round 20: *Sc2tog, sc in next st, repeat from * around, join, ch 1. (20 sts)

Round 21: Sc in each st around, join, ch 1.

At this point attach the safety eyes between rounds 9 and 10 (about 9 stitches apart). Then stuff before closing the head.

Round 22: Sc2tog around, join, ch 1. (10 sts)

Round 23: Sc2tog around, join. (5 sts)

Fasten off leaving a long tail.

Use long tail to close final round and weave in ends.

Use long tail of body to sew on head.

Snout:

With White yarn, create a magic ring, ch 1 and make 10 sc in ring, join to first sc, ch 1.

Round 2: 2 sc in each st around, join, ch 1. (20 sts)

Round 3: Sc in each st around, join, ch 1.

Round 4: *2 sc in next st, sc in next st, repeat from * around, join, ch 1. (30 sts)

Rounds 5–7: Sc in each st around, join, ch 1.

Fasten off leaving a long tail.

Stuff and sew onto front of head, directly under eyes.

Legs (make 2):

With Baby Pink yarn, create a magic ring, ch 1 and make 6 sc in ring, join to first sc, ch 1.

Round 2: 2 sc in each st around, join, ch 2. (12 sts)

Round 3: 2 dc in first 3 sts, 2 hdc in next 2 sts, 2 sc in next 5 sts, 2 hdc in last 2 sts, join, ch 1. (24 sts)

Round 4: Working in back loops only for this round, sc in each st around, join, *change to White yarn*, ch 1.

Rounds 5–6: Sc in each st around, join, ch 1.

Round 7: Sc2tog 6 times, sc in remaining 12 sts, join, ch 1. (18 sts)

Round 8: Sc in each st around, join, ch 1.

Round 9: Sc2tog 5 times, sc in remaining 8 sts, join, ch 1. (13 sts)

Rounds 10–14: Sc in each st around, join, ch 1.

Fasten off leaving a long tail and stuff.

Use long tail to sew onto bottom of body.

Arms (make 2):

With Baby Pink yarn, create a magic ring, ch 1 and make 10 sc in ring, join to first sc, ch 1.

Round 2: *2 sc in next st, sc in next st, repeat from * around, join, ch 1. (15 sts)

Rounds 3–4: Sc in each st around, join, ch 1.

Round 5: *Sc2tog, sc in next 3 sts, repeat from * around, join, *change to White yarn*, ch 1. (12 sts)

Rounds 6–22: Sc in each st around, join, ch 1.

Fasten off leaving a long tail and stuff.

Flatten opening and use long tail to sew onto body under the head.

Ears (make 2):

With White yarn, ch 5, sc in second ch from hook and in remaining 3 chs, ch 1, turn. (4 sts)

Row 2: 2 sc in first st, sc in next 2 sts, 2 sc in last st, ch 1, turn. (6 sts)

Rows 3–5: Sc in each st across, ch 1, turn.

Row 6: Sc2tog, sc in next 2 sts, sc2tog, ch 1, turn. (4 sts)

Row 7: Sc in each st across, ch 1, turn.

Row 8: Sc2tog twice, then continue to sc around entire ear, join to the second sc, causing the ear to cup.

Fasten off leaving a long tail and sew onto head.

Horn:

With Bright Yellow yarn, create a magic ring, ch 1 and make 4 sc in ring, do not join. Continue to work in spiral form without joining or ch 1 until indicated. Use a removable stitch marker to indicate beginning of round if needed.

Round 2: Sc in each st around.

Round 3: *2 sc in next st, sc in next st, repeat from * around. (6 sts)

Round 4: Sc in each st around.

Round 5: *2 sc in next st, sc in next 2 sts, repeat from * around. (8 sts)

Round 6: Sc in each st around.

Round 7: *2 sc in next st, sc in next 3 sts, repeat from * around. (10 sts)

Round 8: Sc in each st around.

Fasten off leaving a long tail and stuff.

Use long tail to sew onto head, centered between eyes and about 4 rounds up.

Hair Coils (make 4 of each color, except White):

Ch 25, 2 sc in second ch from hook and all remaining chs, then fasten off leaving a long tail.

Use long tail to attach 3 coils of each color along top and back of head and 1 coil in each color on the bottom back of body for the tail.

VICTOR THE *Viper*

Ssslithering into your amigurumi collection is the very cute viper snake named Victor! He's a not-so-scary snake, super cute and cuddly!

Size: 24 inches long x 5 inches wide

Materials:
- Bernat Super Value Yarn in Lush
- Bernat Super Value Yarn in Berry
- Size H Crochet Hook
- 12mm Safety Eyes
- Poly-fil Fiber Stuffing
- Tapestry Needle

Head and Body:

With Lush yarn, create a magic ring, ch 1 and make 10 sc in ring, join to first sc, ch 1.

Round 2: 2 sc in each st around, join, ch 1. (20 sts)

Round 3: Sc in each st around, join, ch 1.

Round 4: *2 sc in next st, sc in next st, repeat from * around, join, ch 1. (30 sts)

Round 5: Sc in each st around, join, ch 1.

Round 6: *2 sc in next st, sc in next 2 sts, repeat from * around, join, ch 1. (40 sts)

Round 7: *2 sc in next st, sc in next 3 sts, repeat from * around, join, ch 1. (50 sts)

Rounds 8–15: Sc in each st around, join, ch 1.

Round 16: *Sc2tog, sc in next 3 sts, repeat from * around, join, ch 1. (40 sts)

Round 17: Sc in each st around, join, ch 1.

Round 18: *Sc2tog, sc in next 2 sts, repeat from * around, join, ch 1. (30 sts)

Round 19: Sc in each st around, join, ch 1.

Round 20: *Sc2tog, sc in next st, repeat from * around, join, ch 1. (20 sts)

At this point attach the safety eyes. Then stuff the head and continue as you go, stuffing the head firmly and lightly stuffing the skinny body portion.

Rounds 21–76: Sc in each st around, join, ch 1.

Round 77: *Sc2tog, sc in next 2 sts, repeat from * around, join, ch 1. (15 sts)

Rounds 78–79: Sc in each st around, join, ch 1.

Round 80: *Sc2tog, sc in next st, repeat from * around, join, ch 1. (10 sts)

Rounds 81–84: Sc in each st around, join, ch 1.

Round 85: Sc2tog around, join. (5 sts)

Fasten off leaving a long tail.

Use long tail to close final round and weave in ends.

Tongue:

With Berry yarn, ch 3, sc in second ch from hook and next ch, ch 1, turn. (2 sts)

Rows 2–4: Sc in each st across, ch 1, turn.

Row 5: Sc in each st across, turn.

Row 6: Ch 3, sl st in second ch from hook, sc in next ch, join to first sc in row, ch 3, sl st in second ch from hook, sc in next ch, join to last sc.

Fasten off leaving a long tail and sew tongue onto center front of head.

WALTER THE *Whale*

Walter the Whale may be blue but he is the happiest whale in the ocean! Always flipping his tail fin, he's as friendly as can be. Stitch up this nautical cutie for a whale of a good time!

Size: 13 inches long x 5 inches wide

Materials:

- Bernat Super Value Yarn in Aqua
- Bernat Super Value Yarn in White
- Size H Crochet Hook
- 12mm Safety Eyes
- Poly-fil Fiber Stuffing
- Tapestry Needle

Body:

With Aqua yarn, create a magic ring, ch 1 and make 10 sc in ring, join to first sc, ch 1.

Round 2: 2 sc in each st around, join, ch 1. (20 sts)

Round 3: *2 sc in next st, sc in next st, repeat from * around, join, ch 1. (30 sts)

Round 4: Sc in each st around, join, ch 1.

Round 5: *2 sc in next st, sc in next 2 sts, repeat from * around, join, ch 1. (40 sts)

Round 6: Sc in each st around, join, ch 1.

Round 7: *2 sc in next st, sc in next 3 sts, repeat from * around, join, ch 1. (50 sts)

Rounds 8–19: Sc in each st around, join, ch 1.

Round 20: *Sc2tog, sc in next 3 sts, repeat from * around, join, ch 1. (40 sts)

Rounds 21–22: Sc in each st around, join, ch 1.

Round 23: *Sc2tog, sc in next 2 sts, repeat from * around, join, ch 1. (30 sts)

Rounds 24–25: Sc in each st around, join, ch 1.

Round 26: *Sc2tog, sc in next st, repeat from * around, join, ch 1. (20 sts)

At this point attach the safety eyes, about 15 rounds down and centered on each side of head. Then begin stuffing the head and continue to stuff as you go.

Rounds 27–35: Sc in each st around, join, ch 1.

Round 36: *Sc2tog, sc in next 2 sts, repeat from * around, join, ch 1. (15 sts)

Rounds 37–38: Sc in each st around, join, ch 1.

Round 39: *Sc2tog, sc in next st, repeat from * around, join, ch 1. (10 sts)

Round 40: Sc in each st around, join.

Fasten off leaving a long tail.

Use long tail to close final round and weave in ends.

Tail (make 2 pieces):

With Aqua yarn, create a magic ring, ch 1 and make 6 sc in ring, join to first sc, ch 1.

Round 2: Sc in each st around, join, ch 1.

Round 3: *2 sc in next st, sc in next st, repeat from * around, join, ch 1. (9 sts)

Round 4: Sc in each st around, join, ch 1.

Round 5: *2 sc in next st, sc in next 2 sts, repeat from * around, join, ch 1. (12 sts)

Round 6: *2 sc in next st, sc in next 3 sts, repeat from * around, join, ch 1. (15 sts)

Rounds 7–9: Sc in each st around, join, ch 1.

Round 10: *Sc2tog, sc in next 3 sts, repeat from * around, join, ch 1. (12 sts)

Round 11: *Sc2tog, sc in next 2 sts, repeat from * around, join, ch 1. (9 sts)

Round 12: Sc in each st around, join.

Fasten off leaving a long tail.

Stuff lightly and use long tail to sew tail pieces directly next to each other onto end of body.

Fins (make 2):

With Aqua yarn, create a magic ring, ch 1 and make 10 sc in ring, join to first sc, ch 1.

Round 2: *2 sc in next st, sc in next st, repeat from * around, join, ch 1. (15 sts)

Rounds 3–5: Sc in each st around, join, ch 1.

Fasten off leaving a long tail and sew onto each side of body, about 3 rounds back from the eyes. No need to stuff.

Belly:

With White yarn, ch 11, sc in second ch from hook and the remaining 9 chs, ch 1, turn. (10 sts)

Row 2: 2 sc in first st, sc in next 8 sts, 2 sc in last st, ch 1, turn. (12 sts)

Rows 3–6: Sc in each st across, ch 1, turn.

Row 7: Sc2tog, sc in next 8 sts, sc2tog over last 2 sts, ch 1, turn. (10 sts)

Row 8: Sc in each st across, ch 1, turn.

Row 9: Sc2tog, sc in next 6 sts, sc2tog over last 2 sts, ch 1, turn. (8 sts)

Rows 10–13: Sc in each st across, ch 1, turn.

Row 14: Sc2tog, sc in next 4 sts, sc2tog over last 2 sts, ch 1, turn. (6 sts)

Row 15: Sc2tog, sc in next 2 sts, sc2tog over last 2 sts, ch 1, turn. (4 sts)

Rows 16–29: Sc in each st across, ch 1, turn.

Row 30: Sc2tog twice, then continue to sc around all edges of the belly, join to first sc.

Fasten off leaving a long tail and sew onto belly area of body.

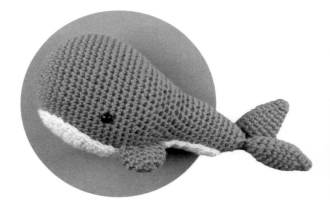

XAVIER THE *X-Ray Fish*

The X-ray fish is typically known for its translucent body, and in this case you can see his backbone in a lighter purple! You can stitch up a whole school.

Size: 13 inches long x 6 inches tall

Materials:
- Bernat Super Value Yarn in Lilac (light purple)
- Bernat Super Value Yarn in Light Damson (dark purple)
- 12mm Safety Eyes
- Poly-fil Fiber Stuffing
- Tapestry Needle

Fish Body:

With Lilac yarn, create a magic ring, ch 1 and make 10 sc in ring, join to first sc, ch 1.

Round 2: 2 sc in each st around, join, ch 1. (20 sts)

Round 3: *2 sc in next st, sc in next st, repeat from * around, join, ch 1. (30 sts)

Round 4: Sc in each st around, join, ch 1.

Round 5: *2 sc in next st, sc in next 2 sts, repeat from * around, join, ch 1. (40 sts)

Round 6: Sc in each st around, join, ch 1.

Round 7: *2 sc in next st, sc in next 3 sts, repeat from * around, join, ch 1. (50 sts)

Rounds 8–9: Sc in each st around, join, ch 1.

Round 10: Sc in each st around, join, *change to Light Damson yarn*, ch 1.

At this point attach the safety eyes on either side of head, between rounds 7 and 8. Stuff the head and continue to stuff as you go.

Rounds 11–20: Sc in each st around, join, ch 1.

Round 21: *Sc2tog, sc in next 8 sts, repeat from * around, join, ch 1. (45 sts)

Round 22: Sc in each st around, join, ch 1.

Round 23: *Sc2tog, sc in next 7 sts, repeat from * around, join, ch 1. (40 sts)

Round 24: Sc in each st around, join, ch 1.

Round 25: *Sc2tog, sc in next 6 sts, repeat from * around, join, ch 1. (35 sts)

Round 26: Sc in each st around, join, ch 1.

Round 27: *Sc2tog, sc in next 5 sts, repeat from * around, join, ch 1. (30 sts)

Round 28: Sc in each st around, join, ch 1.

Round 29: *Sc2tog, sc in next 4 sts, repeat from * around, join, ch 1. (25 sts)

Round 30: Sc in each st around, join, ch 1.

Round 31: *Sc2tog, sc in next 3 sts, repeat from * around, join, ch 1. (20 sts)

Rounds 32–35: Sc in each st around, join, ch 1.

Round 36: *Sc2tog, sc in next 2 sts, join, ch 1. (15 sts)

Round 37: Sc in each st around, join, ch 1.

Round 38: *Sc2tog, sc in next st, join, ch 1. (10 sts)

Round 39: Sc in each st around, join.

Fasten off leaving a long tail but do not close up body yet.

X-ray Skeleton (make 2):

With Lilac yarn, ch 25, fasten off leaving a long tail.

Ch 12, fasten off leaving a long tail.

Ch 10, fasten off leaving a long tail.

Ch 8, fasten off leaving a long tail.

Ch 6, fasten off leaving a long tail.

Sew the ch 25 down middle of body, then sew the ch 12 closest to the head. Sew it on over the ch 25 so it lies across it and slightly bent into a sideways "V." Then sew on the ch 10, ch 8, and ch 6 in the same manner.

Finish stuffing the body and use long tail to sew the body closed at the end, once you have the skeleton chains sewn on.

Bottom Tail Fins (make 2):

With Lilac yarn, create a magic ring, ch 1 and make 6 sc in ring, join to first sc, ch 1.

Round 2: Sc in each st around, join, ch 1.

Round 3: *2 sc in next st, sc in next st, repeat from * around, join, ch 1. (9 sts)

Round 4: Sc in each st around, join, ch 1.

Round 5: *2 sc in next st, sc in next 2 sts, repeat from * around, join, ch 1. (12 sts)

Round 6: *2 sc in next st, sc in next 3 sts, repeat from * around, join, ch 1. (15 sts)

Rounds 7–9: Sc in each st around, join, ch 1.

Round 10: *Sc2tog, sc in next 3 sts, repeat from * around, join, ch 1. (12 sts)

Round 11: *Sc2tog, sc in next 2 sts, repeat from * around, join, ch 1. (9 sts)

Round 12: Sc in each st around, join.

Fasten off leaving a long tail and stuff.

Use long tail to sew tail pieces directly next to each other on the end of the body.

Top Fin:

With Lilac yarn, create a magic ring, ch 1 and make 6 sc in ring, join to first sc, ch 1.

Round 2: Sc in each st around, join, ch 1.

Round 3: *2 sc in next st, sc in next st, repeat from * around, join, ch 1. (9 sts)

Round 4: Sc in each st around, join, ch 1.

Round 5: *2 sc in next st, sc in next 2 sts, repeat from * around, join, ch 1. (12 sts)

Round 6: Sc in each st around, join, ch 1.

Round 7: 2 sc in first 3 sts, sc in remaining sts, join, ch 1. (15 sts)

Round 8: 2 sc in first 3 sts, sc in remaining sts, join, ch 1. (18 sts)

Round 9: 2 sc in first 3 sts, sc in remaining sts, join, ch 1. (21 sts)

Rounds 10–11: Sc in each st around, join, ch 1.

Fasten off leaving a long tail and stuff.

Use long tail to sew onto top of body.

YOLANDA THE *Yak*

Yolanda the Yak is ready to hang out and chat! Known for being big and bulky, this crochet version is cute and cuddly. Stitch up this plush friend complete with shaggy hair and soft horns.

Size: 10 inches tall x 8 inches wide

Materials:

- Bernat Super Value Yarn in Taupe (dark brown)
- Bernat Super Value Yarn in Honey (light brown)
- Bernat Super Value Yarn in White
- Size H Crochet Hook
- 12mm Safety Eyes
- Poly-fil Fiber Stuffing
- Tapestry Needle

Body:

With Taupe yarn, create a magic ring, ch 1 and make 10 sc in ring, join to first sc, ch 1.

Round 2: 2 sc in each st around, join, ch 1. (20 sts)

Round 3: *2 sc in next st, sc in next st, repeat from * around, join, ch 1. (30 sts)

Round 4: Sc in each st around, join, ch 1.

Round 5: *2 sc in next st, sc in next 2 sts, repeat from * around, join, ch 1. (40 sts)

Round 6: Sc in each st around, join, ch 1.

Round 7: *2 sc in next st, sc in next 3 sts, repeat from * around, join, ch 1. (50 sts)

Rounds 8–19: Sc in each st around, join, ch 1.

Round 20: *Sc2tog, sc in next 3 sts, repeat from * around, join, ch 1. (40 sts)

Rounds 21–22: Sc in each st around, join, ch 1.

Round 23: *Sc2tog, sc in next 2 sts, repeat from * around, join, ch 1. (30 sts)

Rounds 24–25: Sc in each st around, join, ch 1.

Round 26: *Sc2tog, sc in next st, repeat from * around, join, ch 1. (20 sts)

Rounds 27–28: Sc in each st around, join, ch 1.

Round 29: Sc2tog around, join. (10 sts)

Fasten off leaving a long tail and stuff, leaving top open.

Head:

With Taupe yarn, create a magic ring, ch 1 and make 10 sc in ring, join to first sc, ch 1.

Round 2: 2 sc in each st around, join, ch 1. (20 sts)

Round 3: Sc in each st around, join, ch 1.

Round 4: *2 sc in next st, sc in next st, repeat from * around, join, ch 1. (30 sts)

Round 5: Sc in each st around, join, ch 1.

Round 6: *2 sc in next st, sc in next 2 sts, repeat from * around, join, ch 1. (40 sts)

Round 7: *2 sc in next st, sc in next 3 sts, repeat from * around, join, ch 1. (50 sts)

Rounds 8–15: Sc in each st around, join, ch 1.

Round 16: *Sc2tog, sc in next 3 sts, repeat from * around, join, ch 1. (40 sts)

Round 17: Sc in each st around, join, ch 1.

Round 18: *Sc2tog, sc in next 2 sts, repeat from * around, join, ch 1. (30 sts)

Round 19: Sc in each st around, join, ch 1.

Round 20: *Sc2tog, sc in next st, repeat from * around, join, ch 1. (20 sts)

Round 21: Sc in each st around, join, ch 1.

At this point attach the safety eyes. Then stuff before closing the head.

Round 22: Sc2tog around, join, ch 1. (10 sts)

Round 23: Sc2tog around, join. (5 sts)

Fasten off leaving a long tail.

Use long tail to close final round and weave in ends.

Use long tail of body to sew on head.

Snout:

With Honey yarn, create a magic ring, ch 1 and make 10 sc in ring, join to first sc, ch 1.

Round 2: 2 sc in each st around, join, ch 1. (20 sts)

Round 3: Sc in each st around, join, ch 1.

Round 4: *2 sc in next st, sc in next st, repeat from * around, join, ch 1. (30 sts)

Rounds 5–7: Sc in each st around, join, ch 1.

Fasten off leaving a long tail.

Stuff and use long tail to sew onto front of head directly under eyes.

Legs (make 2):

With Honey yarn, create a magic ring, ch 1 and make 6 sc in ring, join to first sc, ch 1.

Round 2: 2 sc in each st around, join, ch 2. (12 sts)

Round 3: 2 dc in first 3 sts, 2 hdc in next 2 sts, 2 sc in next 5 sts, 2 hdc in last 2 sts, join, ch 1. (24 sts)

Round 4: Working in back loops only for this round, sc in each st around, join, *change to Taupe yarn*, ch 1.

Rounds 5–6: Sc in each st around, join, ch 1.

Round 7: Sc2tog 6 times, sc in remaining 12 sts, join, ch 1. (18 sts)

Round 8: Sc in each st around, join, ch 1.

Round 9: Sc2tog 5 times, sc in remaining 8 sts, join, ch 1. (13 sts)

Rounds 10–14: Sc in each st around, join, ch 1.

Fasten off leaving a long tail and stuff.

Use long tail to sew onto bottom of body.

Arms (make 2):

With Honey yarn, create a magic ring, ch 1 and make 10 sc in ring, join to first sc, ch 1.

Round 2: *2 sc in next st, sc in next st, repeat from * around, join, ch 1. (15 sts)

Rounds 3–4: Sc in each st around, join, ch 1.

Round 5: *Sc2tog, sc in next 3 sts, repeat from * around, join, *change to Taupe yarn*, ch 1. (12 sts)

Rounds 6–22: Sc in each st around, join, ch 1.

Fasten off leaving a long tail and stuff.

Flatten opening and use long tail to sew onto body under the head.

Horns (make 2):

With White yarn, create a magic ring, ch 1 and make 4 sc in ring, join to first sc, ch 1.

Round 2: *2 sc in next st, sc in next st, repeat from * around, join, ch 1. (6 sts)

Round 3: Sc in each st around, join, ch 1.

Round 4: *2 sc in next st, sc in next 2 sts, repeat from * around, join, ch 1. (8 sts)

Round 5: Sc in each st around, join, ch 1.

Round 6: *2 sc in next st, sc in next 3 sts, repeat from * around, join, ch 1. (10 sts)

Round 7: Sc in each st around, join, ch 1.

Round 8: Sc2tog, sc in each remaining st, ch 1, turn. (9 sts)

Rounds 9–10: Sc in each st around, join, ch 1.

Fasten off leaving a long tail and stuff.

Use long tail to sew onto sides of head.

Ears (make 2):

With Honey yarn, ch 5, sc in second ch from hook and in remaining 3 chs, ch 1, turn. (4 sts)

Row 2: 2 sc in first st, sc in next 2 sts, 2 sc in last st, ch 1, turn. (6 sts)

Rows 3–5: Sc in each st across, ch 1, turn.

Row 6: Sc2tog, sc in next 2 sts, sc2tog over last 2 sts, ch 1, turn. (4 sts)

Row 7: Sc in each st across, ch 1, turn.

Row 8: Sc2tog twice, then continue to sc around entire ear, join to the second sc, causing the ear to cup.

Fasten off leaving a long tail and sew onto head under horns.

Tail:

With Taupe yarn, ch 11, sl st in second ch from hook and the remaining 9 chs, fasten off.

Knot 4 strands of Taupe yarn through last ch so that when knotted it makes a short tassel of 8 strands.

Sew onto back bottom of body.

Hair:

Cut 30 strands of Taupe yarn about 12 inches long. Insert hook through a st on the top of head, then hook center of a single 12-inch strand of yarn and pull through. Now hook the 2 ends of the yarn and pull through the loop. Pull tight. Continue in this manner all around top of head, creating about 30 double strands. Trim yarn after entire hair mane is finished to even out.

ZINA THE *Zebra*

Single crochet stitches and lots of black and white stripes are what Zina the Zebra is made with! Don't let the color changes intimidate you. You can carry your yarn along the inside of the project as you go—no need to clip off and reattach for each round!

Size: 10 inches tall x 8 inches wide

Materials:

- Bernat Super Value Yarn in White
- Bernat Super Value Yarn in Black
- Size H Crochet Hook
- 12mm Safety Eyes
- Poly-fil Fiber Stuffing
- Tapestry Needle

Body:

With White yarn, create a magic ring, ch 1 and make 10 sc in ring, join to first sc, ch 1.

Round 2: 2 sc in each st around, join, ch 1. (20 sts)

Round 3: *2 sc in next st, sc in next st, repeat from * around, join, ch 1. (30 sts)

Round 4: Sc in each st around, join, ch 1.

Round 5: *2 sc in next st, sc in next 2 sts, repeat from * around, join, ch 1. (40 sts)

Change to Black yarn, then continue to alternate between colors every 2 rounds.

Round 6: Sc in each st around, join, ch 1.

Round 7: *2 sc in next st, sc in next 3 sts, repeat from * around, join, ch 1. (50 sts)

Rounds 8–19: Sc in each st around, join, ch 1.

Round 20: *Sc2tog, sc in next 3 sts, repeat from * around, join, ch 1. (40 sts)

Rounds 21–22: Sc in each st around, join, ch 1.

Round 23: *Sc2tog, sc in next 2 sts, repeat from * around, join, ch 1. (30 sts)

Rounds 24–25: Sc in each st around, join, ch 1.

Round 26: *Sc2tog, sc in next st, repeat from * around, join, ch 1. (20 sts)

Rounds 27–28: Sc in each st around, join, ch 1.

Round 29: Sc2tog around, join. (10 sts)

Fasten off leaving a long tail and stuff, leaving top open.

Head:

Start with White yarn, then continue to alternate between Black and White every 2 rounds.

With White yarn, create a magic ring, ch 1 and make 10 sc in ring, join to first sc, ch 1.

Round 2: 2 sc in each st around, join, ch 1. (20 sts)

Round 3: Sc in each st around, join, ch 1.

Round 4: *2 sc in next st, sc in next st, repeat from * around, join, ch 1. (30 sts)

Round 5: Sc in each st around, join, ch 1.

Round 6: *2 sc in next st, sc in next 2 sts, repeat from * around, join, ch 1. (40 sts)

Round 7: *2 sc in next st, sc in next 3 sts, repeat from * around, join, ch 1. (50 sts)

Rounds 8–15: Sc in each st around, join, ch 1.

Round 16: *Sc2tog, sc in next 3 sts, repeat from * around, join, ch 1. (40 sts)

Round 17: Sc in each st around, join, ch 1.

Round 18: *Sc2tog, sc in next 2 sts, repeat from * around, join, ch 1. (30 sts)

Round 19: Sc in each st around, join, ch 1.

Round 20: *Sc2tog, sc in next st, repeat from * around, join, ch 1. (20 sts)

Change to White and continue in White to end.

Round 21: Sc in each st around, join, ch 1.

At this point attach the safety eyes between rounds 9 and 10 (about 9 sts apart). Then stuff before closing the head.

Round 22: Sc2tog around, join, ch 1. (10 sts)

Round 23: Sc2tog around, join. (5 sts)

Fasten off leaving a long tail.

Use long tail to close final round and weave in ends.

Use long tail of body to sew on head.

Snout:

With Black yarn, create a magic ring, ch 1 and make 10 sc in ring, join to first sc, ch 1.

Round 2: 2 sc in each st around, join, ch 1. (20 sts)

Round 3: Sc in each st around, join, ch 1.

Round 4: *2 sc in next st, sc in next st, repeat from * around, join, ch 1. (30 sts)

Rounds 5–7: Sc in each st around, join, ch 1.

Fasten off leaving a long tail.

Stuff and use long tail to sew onto front of head directly under eyes.

Legs (make 2):

With Black yarn, create a magic ring, ch 1 and make 6 sc in ring, join to first sc, ch 1.

Round 2: 2 sc in each st around, join, ch 2. (12 sts)

Round 3: 2 dc in first 3 sts, 2 hdc in next 2 sts, 2 sc in next 5 sts, 2 hdc in last 2 sts, join, ch 1. (24 sts)

Round 4: Working in back loops only for this round, sc in each st around, join, ch 1.

Change to White yarn, then continue to alternate between colors every 2 rounds.

Rounds 5–6: Sc in each st around, join, ch 1.

Round 7: Sc2tog 6 times, sc in remaining 12 sts, join, ch 1. (18 sts)

Round 8: Sc in each st around, join, ch 1.

Round 9: Sc2tog 5 times, sc in remaining 8 sts, join, ch 1. (13 sts)

Rounds 10–14: Sc in each st around, join, ch 1.

Fasten off leaving a long tail and stuff.

Use long tail to sew onto bottom of body.

Arms (make 2):

With Black yarn, create a magic ring, ch 1 and make 10 sc in ring, join to first sc, ch 1.

Round 2: *2 sc in first st, sc in next st, repeat from * around, join, ch 1. (15 sts)

Rounds 3–4: Sc in each st around, join, ch 1.

Round 5: *Sc2tog, sc in next 3 sts, repeat from * around, join, ch 1. (12 sts)

Change to White yarn, then continue to alternate between colors every 2 rounds.

Rounds 6–22: Sc in each st around, join, ch 1.

Fasten off leaving a long tail and stuff.

Flatten opening and use long tail to sew onto body under the head.

Ears (make 2):

With White yarn, ch 5, sc in second ch from hook and in remaining 3 chs, ch 1, turn. (4 sts)

Row 2: 2 sc in first st, sc in next 2 sts, 2 sc in last st, ch 1, turn. (6 sts)

Rows 3–5: Sc in each st across, ch 1, turn.

Row 6: Sc2tog, sc in next 2 sts, sc2tog over last 2 sts, ch 1, turn. (4 sts)

Row 7: Sc in each st across, ch 1, turn.

Row 8: Sc2tog twice, then continue to sc around entire ear, join to the second sc, causing the ear to cup.

Fasten off leaving a long tail and sew onto head.

Tail:

With Black yarn, ch 11, sl st in second ch from hook and the remaining 9 chs, fasten off.

Knot 2 strands of Black yarn through last ch so that when knotted it makes a short tassel of 4 strands.

Sew onto back bottom of body.

Hair:

Cut 52 strands of Black yarn about 12 inches long. Insert hook through a st on the top of head, then hook center of a single 12-inch strand of yarn and pull through. Now hook the 2 ends of the yarn and pull through the loop. Pull tight. Repeat, creating about 13 rows of the mane, each row 4 strands across. Trim yarn after entire hair mane is finished to even out.

INDEX

ACKNOWLEDGMENTS

First and foremost, I would like to thank the crochet community for all of their continued support. Each and every one of you that has followed me through my blog and social channels has kept me motivated with your positive comments and feedback. It means more than you will ever know! Loving my crochet projects and sharing them others is the greatest compliment I could ever receive.

To my fellow crochet designers and blogging buddies . . . thank you for being a shoulder to lean on and for your guidance over the years. You understand this niche. You love yarn as much as I do, and it's so nice to be surrounded by people who get what you do and to feel the love and support.

Thank you to Spinrite Yarns for providing all of the yarn I needed to write this book and design each of the cute critters! To the Yarnspirations marketing team . . . thank you for always being an e-mail or phone call away. Your unwavering support over the last four years has meant a ton.

I would like to thank the entire team at Callisto Media for being an absolutely amazing partner through this journey. To Salwa, my senior editor, who has been with me every step of the way, to all of the editors, proofreaders, designers, and photographers . . . thank you for your contribution in making this book a reality!

Thank you to my parents for their faith in me. Thank you for letting me pursue my love of arts and crafts from a very young age. Mom, you have always been my sounding board and my best friend. Dad, you are my role model, teaching me how to build a business from the ground up. Just like you did! I love you both and can't thank you enough for helping to shape me into the person I am today.

To my husband, Joel, thank you for being my rock. I appreciate your love and support from the moment I came up with the idea to start a blog and crochet business. You've always been my biggest cheerleader. I love you!

Thank you to my children. My greatest joys in life, you are also the inspiration behind so many of my designs: my oldest son, Micah, who is so incredibly smart and always eager and willing to help; my middle son, Chase, who is the funniest and most creative person I've ever met; and my daughter, Zoe, who is the best crochet model and sidekick I could ever ask for! This book is for the three of you!

And thank you to my extended family and friends, who have always believed in me and encouraged my creativity, love of crafts, yarn, and art. You know who you are and the role you've played in guiding my path. Thank you!

ABOUT THE AUTHOR

Sarah Zimmerman is a yarn lover, crafter, blogger, wife, and busy stay-at-home mom of three. Sarah is a self-taught crocheter who picked up her first hook shortly after her second child was born. Wanting to make fun hats for her kids, she watched online videos and followed book tutorials, learning to crochet quickly and unleashing a hidden talent she never knew she had! She decided to take her hobby and passion for crochet to the next level and started writing her own patterns. A graduate of the University of Washington with a degree in visual arts and a graphic designer by trade, Sarah has an eye for design and color that is reflected in her crochet projects. Her style can be described as fresh, cute, and contemporary with a creative flair that appeals to all ages. You will find many of her patterns are easy to adapt, and many incorporate additional craft materials like fleece, buttons, and felt. Sarah's craft and crochet blog, *Repeat Crafter Me*, is full of new and unique patterns that are trendy and seasonal, as well as many animal and character hats for babies and kids. She offers simple, free patterns and is known for having easy-to-follow tutorials and detailed step-by-step photos. She loves crafting with her kids, taking on DIY projects, experimenting in the kitchen, and is never far from her crochet hook and a ball of yarn.

Website: www.RepeatCrafterMe.com
E-mail: RepeatCrafterMe@gmail.com
Facebook: www.facebook.com/repeatcrafterme
Instagram: @repeatcrafterme

NOTES

NOTES

NOTES

NOTES